# Who Do You Say I Am?

*Personal Life Stories Told by the LGBTQ Community*

*Many blessings*
*CGibbs*

## Carol Marchant Gibbs

Published by 89th Street Publishers, LLC in the United States. For bulk orders contact *89thstreetpublishers@gmail.com*.

FIRST EDITION

Book cover design by Peter O'Connor, *BespokeBookCovers.com*. Interior design and formation by Lorna Lee, *LornasVoice.com*. Editing by Amy King.

ISBN 978-1-7320715-0-6

Library of Congress Cataloging-in-Publication Data to be applied for.

2 4 6 8 10 9 7 5 3 1

# *Dedication*

To the One from whom this message of love has
come. Thank you, God, for
entrusting me with this very important word. May
Your voice be heard, and may You get all the honor and
glory that you deserve.

# *Acknowledgements*

To those of you from the LGBTQ community who were courageous enough to share your stories, it has been a privilege to be invited into the depths of your lives. Your stories were a beautiful gift. Thank you. I am profoundly grateful for the amazing encouragement that I have received from family and friends while writing this book.

Thank you to those of you who reviewed my very rough draft and took time to respond with honest words and gentle recommendations. Thank you, Leigh, Dick, Sheldon, Marc, and Laurie.

To Amy King, my primary editor. Thank you for your heart to see and speak into the compassionate message of love that I was trying to communicate. To Heidi, many thanks for getting the editing process started.

Many thanks to the very creative Peter O'Connor from Bespoke Book Covers. You helped to communicate the heart behind this book...life anew.

I could not be more thankful for the amazing efforts of Lorna Lee Earl. Charged with formatting this book, you went way beyond the call using your editing expertise and encouragement to bring us to this point.

To my niece, Ashley, thank you for the ways you have expanded my ability to love.

To my loving son, Jamey, incredible daughter-in-law, Katie, and precious grandchildren, life with you has been one of my greatest joys. Thank you for the ways you have prayed for us and loved us through all the seasons of life. You have celebrated each step in this process and encouraged me daily.

To my wonderful son-in-law, Leandro, thank you for sharing your storytelling expertise through kind words of encouragement and constructive feedback. You inspired me to press through the many, many, many editing changes. You have not only been a gift to this book but are a gift to our family.

To my amazing son, Jeremy, without your courage to come out, I am not sure if any of this would have happened. God has used you to reveal a deeper love. Thank you for all that you have taught me that has broadened my understanding and given me a greater sensitivity to the LGBTQ community. Your heart for people and passion for justice is contagious. I am so proud of the man you have become.

To my partner in life, my husband and friend, Jim. You have been my biggest fan. You have prayed for me, encouraged, and advised me. You have been my reviewer of contracts, editor, marketing agent, and personal chef. Thank you for your love and support not only for this book, but throughout our forty years of marriage. I love you with all my heart.

# *Table of Contents*

# *Glossary*

*LGBTQ*—An acronym for "lesbian, gay, bisexual, transgender and queer."

**L:** *Lesbian*—A woman who is emotionally, romantically or sexually attracted to other women.

**G:** *Gay*—A person who is emotionally, romantically or sexually attracted to members of the same gender.

**B:** *Bi-Sexual*—A person emotionally, romantically or sexually attracted to more than one sex, gender or gender identity though not necessarily simultaneously.

**T:** *Transgender*—A term used for people whose gender identity and/or expression is different from cultural expectations based on the sex they were assigned at birth. Being transgender does not imply any specific sexual orientation. Therefore, transgender people may identify as straight, gay, lesbian, bisexual, etc.

**Q:** *Queer*—A term people often use to express fluid identities and orientations.

Other terms:

*Gender Identity*—One's own innermost concept of self as male, female, a blend of both or neither. How individuals perceive themselves. One's gender identity can be the same or different from their sex assigned at birth.

*Closeted*—Describes an LGBTQ person who has not disclosed their sexual orientation or gender identity.

*Gender Transition*—The process by which some people strive to more closely align their internal knowledge of gender with its outward appearance. Some people socially transition, whereby they might begin dressing, using names and pronouns and/or be socially recognized as another gender. Others undergo physical transitions in which they modify their bodies through medical interventions.

*Outing*—Exposing someone's lesbian, gay, bisexual or transgender identity to others without their permission.

*Pan Sexual*—A person who is attracted to others regardless of their gender identity or biological sex.

*Sexual Orientation*—An inherent or emotional, romantic or sexual attraction to other people.

# *Prologue*

There once was a deeply compassionate man who had such a heart for his country that he committed his life to bringing good mental health to those whom God put before him in the army. He married a wonderful woman who supported him in everything he did. They spent their lives moving their family from army base to army base where the man served. Early in their marriage, the man spent a year in Korea during the war, working at a MASH unit that provided support to those on the front line. The man and woman made many sacrifices through the years, but when they share of their army days, their eyes light up and they smile. The memories are amazing treasures...except for one.

One night, during the man's time in the service, a dear friend came to the man and woman to share a very deep secret. Brian had been a close friend of theirs for a long time. He was also a psychiatrist and worked closely alongside the man. The man and the woman often had dinner at Brian's home, and they would return the favor by inviting Brian to theirs. They loved him. This particular night, Brian arrived physically beaten up and grief-stricken. He explained that he had been arrested during his time off and was asked by the army to retire early. No one really knew the details that led to such drastic measures but they did know this: Brian was secretly gay. Everyone knew he was gay, but they never talked about it because they believed it was the loving thing to do. They thought that helping him keep his secret was a means of protecting him. The man and woman lovingly listened to Brian as he shared about his life. They comforted him that night. Then, he went home and the three of them never talked about it again.

Over the next few months, Brian went through the normal retirement process. His secret continued to be kept and Brian's grief about his life grew into a deep despair. After the entire process of separating from the military was completed, one dark night, Brian took his own life. The man and woman were devastated as were all of Brian's other friends. Their greatest regret was not talking honestly with him, hearing his story, and telling him how much he was loved by them and by God. From that point on, more than ever, they committed their lives to loving well those whom God put before them...especially members of the gay community.

I have great admiration for my father-in-law and mother-in-law. They were always very kind and compassionate people. But, I never understood their position on same-sex attraction until I heard the story of Brian. God changed them the day Brian died. Their hearts grew a greater capacity to love.

Their story was told to me by our younger son, Jeremy, shortly after he came out. His grandparents had shared it with him when he told them his story. On hearing about Brian from our son, I swore that I would do whatever it took to love him well. Taking one's life should never be an answer...love is.

# *My Story*

## Chapter 1

Eleven years ago, God changed my life in an extraordinary way in response to a prayer, "Lord, please help me to love well."

I had given much thought to what it looked like to love well. It seemed like such a simple prayer but it was answered differently than I anticipated. I expected that God would increase my number of lunch dates to encourage people, or have me support them through difficult life circumstances, but God had deep transformational ideas in mind in response to my naive invitation. So, when I prayed to love well, God presented me with three very unexpected and powerful experiences, over a few short months.

First, my husband was invited to consider a position on staff at our church to be the director of International Ministries. It was an amazing position, so after much prayer, he left a very lucrative position as a lawyer to go to a not so financially lucrative position at church. It was a calling from God. I joined him on staff a year later.

Then, my father was diagnosed with terminal lung cancer. I stepped down from my new teaching position to help care for him, along with my siblings, until he died seven months later. It was a heartrending experience.

The third experience took us to our knees. Our younger son, who was twenty-two at the time, told us he believed he was gay. He was not certain and invited our family to join him on a journey to discern. He explained that he had been experiencing same-sex attraction for ten years prior and asked us to pray for him as he questioned God about his identity. "Is this who I really am?" Our son chose to go through counseling during this process and spent the next couple of months in prayer and discernment with a young couple from the Christian organization that had mentored him in college. They walked with him through the Bible exploring original text to see what God had said about same-sex attraction. I was convinced that he would come out of this process believing that he was straight. That was not the result of his discernment. After months, of seeking answers, he believed that this was who God created him to be…a gay man. We were devastated.

How could this be? Both of our sons were raised in the church and had been very active in it as leaders. When they went to college, they found a home in the Christian organization on campus. Our younger son was president, for heaven's sake. My husband and I began to pray for God to step in and show Himself strong, and He did… but not the way we expected.

I was raised in the church at a time where what was taught went unquestioned. And, what was taught about the LGBTQ community stayed with me for a very long time; that being gay was a wrong choice.

The months following my son's declaration, my husband and I spent many hours with him sharing everything that we believed, everything that the church had taught us about being gay. We quoted bible verses and shared our opinions about something we knew *nothing* about, hoping that we could convince him otherwise. It was not our finest hour as parents.

Then, we began to examine ourselves. When something occurs in the life of your children you are forced to question if you were in anyway responsible. Our sons were raised in a Christian home. They went to Sunday school, went through all the youth groups, and committed their lives to Christ. What had we done, or not done, that had contributed to his being gay? It was a very humbling experience.

To say that our world was rocked does not even come close to the immense emotions that we experienced during this time. All the hopes and dreams that we had for our younger son were dashed in an instant...and we struggled for answers. We wanted to protect him from the world's response. The thought of him having a lifetime of persecution was heartbreaking. What about marriage? What about grandchildren...our grandchildren?

Our older son, sixteen and a half months older than his brother, had just married a wonderful young woman a few months before. She was our younger son's best friend in high school. Our younger son would never have this in his life. What about his future? Where was God in all of this? Wasn't He supposed to be sovereign? Why wasn't He doing anything?

Over the next few months, there were many conversations as a family and with God. There were many sleepless nights and many tears shed.

Then…one day…God spoke. He said that our response to our son was to "just love him." God had plans. He would take care of him.

"This is what loving well looks like."

So, as God began to reveal more of His love for our family, my husband and I began to do research on same-sex attraction and our eyes were opened. We started to think differently, and we slowly began to realize that we had been prepared for this very moment in time.

ଓ ଓ ଓ

Our life experiences have been both joyful and challenging, but all have helped to build our capacity to love. Let me take you on our journey.

I say, "our journey," because my husband and I have been married for over forty years. It is hard to remember my life without him. We met in high school and remained casual friends for the year that we were in school together. He was two years older than me, graduated and went off to the Naval Academy while I finished high school and started college. We would see each other occasionally when he would visit home and attend our church. We dated for a short period of time while he was at the Naval Academy, but I ended it when it was clear that he was far more serious about me than I him. He laughs and denies when I tell this story but it is true. He was crazy about me.

One year later, I started thinking about him, got his address from his mother and wrote him a letter. This was long before the internet. He had graduated and was stationed in California at the time. The day after I mailed the letter, I received a large photo from him of the Golden Gate Bridge with an invitation to accompany him to a wedding while he was home over Christmas. Our letters had passed in the mail. We got together over Christmas…and the rest is history.

We were engaged four months later and because I was still in college, we did not marry until two and a half years later. We had a beautiful wedding and I followed him to a Naval Base in Charleston, South Carolina, where he was on a nuclear submarine. After being in the Navy for a few more years, it became clear that the personal sacrifice of being separated for long periods of time was something that we did not want to continue. We admire highly those who serve our country in such a sacrificial way…but it wasn't for us.

We moved to Washington, DC for his last tour of duty and he started applying to law schools. It was a dream come true when the University of Virginia extended an invitation for him to attend. We packed our bags and moved to Charlottesville, VA.

I was working as the assistant manager in a bank in Old Town Alexandria at the time. We were so grateful that the bank transferred me to a Charlottesville branch into a position overseeing the bookkeeping department. I was totally unqualified for the job but after sitting with every person that I was responsible for to learn their tasks, I was up to speed. I loved it. It was challenging and fun.

My husband and I had always wanted children. I was ready the minute we were married. I used to think that bringing children into this world was a given. My mother had five children and I assumed that the simplicity with which that happened for her would translate to what I would experience. It did not...until law school.

We had been married three years and were three months into law school when we discovered that we were going to be parents the following August. This was an amazing surprise. We were over the moon excited! The fact that I was our sole provider at the time (with a little money from Naval Reserves and a student loan) didn't enter our minds. We knew that God had plans and we embraced this plan with joy.

The pregnancy was a very normal one. I worked full time at the bank and when I wasn't there, I was sleeping on the sofa at the law school library while my husband studied. To me, it was perfect. Somewhere along the pregnancy, we discovered that we were having a girl. Our house was flooded with pink clothing. Some very wise people gave more neutral colors and we decorated the nursery in blue and yellow. We were ready!!

August arrived, and it was the hottest on record...or maybe it just felt that way. We had no air conditioning, so we found ourselves sleeping in the dusty unfinished basement with occasional mice running by...but the anticipation of our daughter made even that acceptable.

My brother got married four days before my due date and the doctor advised that we not travel home for the wedding. It was a three-hour drive at best and he wanted us close. I mourned the fact that I was going to miss that wonderful family event...and stayed home. I remember crying as my husband and I cleaned up our yard that weekend. I think it was outdoor "nesting." But, once again, thoughts of our daughter turned that around.

I had a scheduled doctor's appointment that Monday, the day before my due date. That was a morning that I will never forget. On examination, the doctor was unable to hear the baby's heartbeat. For a moment, I felt like the life drained out of my body. It was devastating!! But, we still had hope that maybe he was wrong. He must have missed something.

The doctor scheduled a sonogram and on the way to the hospital, we stopped at our church, fell to our knees and cried out to God. There was still hope. Sadly, the sonogram confirmed our greatest fears. The baby was no longer living. We returned home to gather everything we would need to go through the ordeal of delivering our baby.

I requested a Cesarean-section so I could be put under anesthesia and be absent for the experience of loss, but the doctor, in his wisdom, advised that we go with our original plan of natural childbirth. He said that the emotional loss would be enough. I did not need the physical reminder. So, my husband and I went through the process of delivering a stillborn child. The hospital staff connected me to Pitocin and labor began. It was like any other delivery. My husband bravely coached me through each contraction. And even still...I believed that God could work a miracle. I desperately needed the medical staff to be wrong.

A few hours later, our daughter was born... still, just as they had expressed. I was not planning to see our baby. I wanted it to be a nightmare from which I would eventually awaken but when my husband expressed his heart to see our daughter, I did the same. She was beautiful and perfect. There was nothing indicating why she was not going to be part of our lives. We were heartbroken. We named her Jessica Ryan…just as we had planned. The doctor had me recover on a floor far from the new mothers. I was grateful to not hear the crying of new babies or the joy of young parents.

Our family came for the funeral two days later. It was one of the saddest moments of my life. We mourned for the sweet child we would never have the privilege of raising. We were changed forever.

I went back to work at the bank sooner than I should have. My body was weak and still healing but I needed to be distracted from our terrible loss. Most people were so kind, expressing sympathy and love for us. Others, in their struggle to know what to say, said nothing. This was the most painful of all. Life was not the same for us...nor would it ever be. We just needed them to say they "were sorry." But they were silent.

I spent the next few months trying to work through the grief. I poured over the Psalms in search of hope. Then...one day, I came to a verse that changed my life. Psalm 4:3 says, "Know that the Lord has set apart the godly for Himself; the Lord will hear when I call to Him." Our daughter had been set apart and God had her with Him. There was hope. We would one day be reunited.

I wish I could say that the next few months were much easier...and they were in some respects. The most difficult part was witnessing poor parenting out in public. I wondered why we were unable to raise our daughter when there were parents who seemed highly bothered by their children…such precious gifts. I confess I spent a great deal of time judging those parents.

Our desire to have and love children intensified to new levels. Twenty months later, I gave birth to our first son. This pregnancy was filled with joy but much anxiety, too. We were involved in three car accidents that were not our fault. It felt like we had a target on our car that said, "two potential new parents in need of testing…hit me." In addition, our first dog, that we dearly loved, was hit by a car and died. I fell in the snow and started bleeding…only to find out I had a bad case of hemorrhoids. Too much information? Each accident prompted a trip to the hospital. Everything was fine. Because of our previous experience, the doctor chose to deliver our son two weeks early. Miraculously, we delivered a healthy beautiful baby boy. James Anthony…named after my husband, his father and my father. He was perfect. We have thanked God every day for giving us such a wonderful gift. Jamey was a very easy baby…sweet natured and joy filled. We were head over heels in love. Life was perfect!!

You can imagine how surprised we were when we discovered that we were once again expecting another baby. I was still nursing our first son…so how could this be? That did explain my immense fatigue, however. I was already three months along in the pregnancy when we discovered this. After we recovered from the shock my husband and I felt exceedingly blessed. The boys would be very close in age 16 1/2 months apart. We were up for the task.

Although my first pregnancy was filled with crazy experiences, our first son was a very easy baby even in utero. He was calm and seemed to do all the things babies in utero do; he moved some and slept.

Our second son was a totally different story. Early in my pregnancy, we discovered that the RH incompatibility that my husband and I shared had become a potential danger for our son. Throughout my pregnancy, the doctor was constantly monitoring the baby by checking the bilirubin level through amniocentesis. There was even talk of an in-utero blood transfusion. Thirty plus years ago, that was a big deal. They just kept repeating that if I could carry him to twenty-eight weeks, he would have a chance. Our medical situation became the focus of a whole team of doctors that were fighting to deliver a healthy baby. It was nerve- racking.

The doctor delivered our second son two weeks early. I was induced on Friday and he arrived on Sunday afternoon. I should have known that this little guy had his own plan and was not going to be swayed otherwise. By Sunday afternoon, the doctor, told me he was going to rupture my membrane (break my water). In his words, "You are committed now. You must deliver the baby or I will have to take him." The minute the doctor left the room, I started feeling like I had to push. I called the nurse who responded to me in a very condescending manner, "Oh honey, he just broke your water. I'm certain you do not have to push yet." I explained that I had done this before, it was not my first rodeo, call the anesthesiologist. I was planning to have anesthesia this time unlike the times before. She left the room unimpressed.

When the nurse returned, I insisted that she check my progress...once again telling her to call the anesthesiologist. She finally did and responded with, "Oh...too late for that!! You are ready to deliver." I confess that I wanted to throttle her at that very moment. The doctor rushed in and after four pushes our new little guy had arrived. Jeremy Jacob. Forty-five minutes after my water was broken.

They checked him over thoroughly. RH incompatibility can cause many serious birth defects. He was beautiful...a little jaundice but that was understandable. Everything else seemed to be fine. Praise God.

After we greeted our new son, the nurses swept him away to be placed under the lights to help with the jaundice. He would come in periodically to feed but spent most of his days under the lights. We did not mind; we were so thankful he had arrived safely.

A pediatric specialist came into our room that same day, explaining that when the RH factor affects a pregnancy, you carry those antibodies forever. Jeremy had arrived with minor effects, but each subsequent child would have more severe issues. It would be a risk to have more children. This is not what we had planned...but we were so thankful he was going to live a healthy life.

The jaundice made it necessary for Jeremy to stay in the hospital a few days after I could return home. Our sixteen-and-a-half-month-old baby, Jamey, was really confused by our absence. We had been gone for five days to have a baby and came home empty handed. He would not even look at me for the first hour. He came around shortly after that.

I spent the next few days running back and forth to the hospital to nurse the baby. My mother-in-law did the shuttling and caring for Jamey. She was a god sent. We were so thankful.

We brought Jeremy home a few days later and our new life with two sons began. Jamey adjusted quickly to life with a brother. He was gentle and kind.

Jeremy was anemic, so the doctors hoped that giving him iron would boost his levels. If you have ever taken iron, you know that it plays havoc on your gastrointestinal system. To say he was very colicky does not even touch the effect the iron had on his little body. He was great while in the snuggly baby carrier and would sleep well there, but the minute we took him out, he was awake. Secretly we had thoughts of hanging the snuggly on the doorknob with him in it...but we didn't. Yes...tired parents think of the craziest things. My husband was an amazing support, taking the "nightshift" so I could sleep in between feedings. I am not sure how he managed during the day at work, but he did.

Two weeks later, we were back in the hospital with Jeremy. The iron was unsuccessful in correcting his anemia, so he was scheduled to receive a pack of red blood cells. We were so thankful for modern medicine. This immediately turned him around. He was in great health. Our concern, however, was that though blood could be tested for many things at that time, it could not be tested for AIDS. We just had to trust that God had him in His care. There was nothing else we could do. God did protect him.

We were informed when Jeremy was born that he had a heart murmur. The doctor's hope was that the hole that caused this would close on its own without needing surgery. We went to a pediatric cardiologist for a year, checking on his progress. Eventually the hole closed up. All was well.

Our years with our two sons have been filled with great joy. The first few years of childbearing really formed us as parents. God used every experience to deepen our ability to love them…and we do. Raising children has been one of God's greatest gifts to us and we are so very thankful.

Our boys have always been a delight. They are different as night and day, but their differences always seemed to complement each other. Their personalities emerged at birth. Our older son was very kind, loving, laid-back, funny, and very compliant. Our younger son was loving, funny, and not at all laid-back. We would say he was "passionate." As a child, he could get into things faster than you could ever imagine. Oh…and the temper tantrums. They were quite the pair. Both boys are pretty much the same today… minus the temper tantrums. And today, they remain even at ages 33 and 34, absolutely-adorable!

Because we raised two boys, it was easy to assume that two boys very close in age would love to be engaged in the same activities. At an early age, we had them involved in gymnastics, baseball, and basketball. For a while, they seemed like they both loved it, always going along happily. It did not take long to figure out that our different children could possibly have different interests. Our older son was quite the athlete and took sports very seriously even at a young age. Our younger son would sit in the outfield lacing wild flowers through his baseball glove. I would call to him, "Get in the game, Jer." He would smile, wave his glove and stand up in the field. Flowers still laced.

On returning home from a business trip, my husband related a conversation that he had with a friend of his that had twins. He spoke about their differences and different interests. The light went on. Our children were still very young, ages four and five, so we didn't totally miss the boat. We started to expose them to a panoply of experiences in hopes that it would reveal a special interest or talent. As we studied our sons' curiosities and talents, we discovered that they did have very different interests. Our boys did not just play sports. The arts became much more a part of our lives and both of our children began to thrive. We really were very attentive parents, so we were shocked that we missed this. It sounds so ridiculously obvious. Our sons were different from day one...really from the womb. So, as our sons grew so did our ability to parent each of them. We tried to focus on them as individuals instead of a team.

When our sons were six and seven years old, our thirteen-year-old niece, Ashley, suddenly moved in with us. Her parents were getting a divorce and it became necessary for her to have another place to live for a while. We loved her and offered to have her move in with us. I remember Jeremy asking me one day, months after she arrived, if "this was why their sister did not live…so Ashley could move in with us?" I thought about that question a lot. Would our hearts have been big enough to share more love? Ashley brought with her much sadness and responded to this serious life event in many dramatic ways for many years following, but she grew up. Becoming a young mom at age nineteen helped to form her and her love for children. She put herself through college and later became a successful pediatric nurse practitioner. We are so proud of her.

Our sons have grown up to be wonderful young men and are still different as night and day. My older son, Jamey, is so much like my husband it is scary… in a good way. He is rather laid back, very kind and has a heart to serve. He does have a little bit of me thrown in. He has a great sense of humor, is extremely witty, and is generally fun to be around. Our younger son, Jeremy, is like a clone of me. He is also very humorous, has a heart for people and a passion to fight injustice. Both boys love deeply. We could not be prouder of them. Raising them has been one of our greatest joys in life.

The reason I am telling you all of this is because our lives have been blessed with great joys and great hardship. Each moment has helped to form us into the people that we are today. So, when Jeremy came out, we were not unfamiliar with life's challenges. We just weren't familiar with this one.

You may ask if we even had a clue that our son was gay. We really did not…we were totally clueless. But, Jeremy would tell you that he began to experience same sex attraction when he was in third grade. He always had many friends but felt differently about the boys then he did the girls. As he grew older, those feelings began to intensify but our involvement in the church encouraged him to ignore what he was feeling. I remember when he was in high school, he expressed to me that he thought he was experiencing same sex attraction and I told him not to worry that "I am sure all boys experience that at some time." God forgive me. His intense feelings continued to be internalized and buried by a sea of church activities. He did date several girls in high school and in college. He is quite adorable so he could pretty much date anyone he chose. All along, he was attempting to be someone he was not.

He majored in psychology in college, I believe to get a deeper understanding of himself, hoping to make sense of his feelings. During his time in college, he began to go to the LGBTQ group on campus. At first, it was to get a better understanding of that community. Then, it became a refuge for him...a place where someone understood. At the same time, he was president of the Christian organization on campus, trying to pray away the feelings that he was having. For ten years, Jeremy attempted to pray away his feelings, living a straight life.

Jeremy came out a year after graduating from college. It was a very difficult time, but God was clearly working in us and around us. He worked hard to reconcile his life as a gay Christian man and God brought opportunities before him to do so.

It was right before Christmas, and he had been communicating with people from an organization called the "Gay Christian Network." This organization was developed to show love and support to gay Christians, to give them a sense of community. There was a conference an hour away and he had decided to attend with some of the friends he had met. Mid-way through the conference, I received a call from Jeremy with a request. He asked if he could bring his friends home for dinner. I will never forget that night. As we sat around that dinner table, my husband and I at one end, Jamey and Katie at the other, along with ten gay men, I was changed. We heard story after story of each life, their hopes and their dreams. All were followers of Christ wanting to embrace their calling; a worship leader, one in seminary, a police officer, someone in film, a social worker, and so on. Some of them had been rejected by the church because of they were honest about their same sex attraction. These were beautiful men who wanted to make a difference in the world. It was that night that God gave me a new heart. I began to see differently. They were kind and compassionate and had a steadfast faith in God that was untainted by the negative responses they had received from the church. I loved these men.

After that experience, my husband and I started sharing more freely with our closest friends and family about our life with Jeremy. We shared with the people closest to us, first. They knew us and loved us. I am so thankful for those people who have walked with us through this journey. Many lives have been changed by our son's coming out and God has showed Himself strong through it all.

There have been challenges along the way but God has been there to remind us of His love for our family. A few years back when "Proposition 6," about marriage equality, came on the docket, our church decided to have forums regarding it. The church shared their position of believing that marriage is to be between one man and one woman. Then, they invited people from an organization that supported therapy that would "re-orient" sexuality. "Reformed" gays came to share their stories. It was heartbreaking. They were so sad and wept as they shared about their lives. There was no joy. The church silently promoted living a celibate life without love.

I left the forums and wept in my car, crying out to God on our son's behalf. What in the world was God doing? And again, God repeated what He had been saying to us all along.

"Just love him. I will take care of the rest." And so, we did...and God has been faithful.

The most recent challenge has been what God has used to inspire me to write this book. At the beginning of 2016, my husband was diagnosed with cancer of the appendix. It is a very rare and extremely aggressive cancer that travels on the surface of organs. It was found during a routine colonoscopy. He had a very extensive ten-hour surgery, eight months of chemotherapy and seems to be doing great. Praise God. He will be monitored often over the next few years.

Just prior to that diagnosis, we had joined our son and son-in-law in Palm Springs to plan their wedding. We were so thankful that our son had fallen in love with such a wonderful man and excited that my husband would officiate the wedding. It was going to be beautiful. There was a lot of prayer poured into that decision to officiate.

Eleven years ago, as we were working through the thick of what it meant to have a gay son, Jeremy asked my husband that if he should ever find someone he wanted to spend the rest of his life with, would he officiate the ceremony. My husband spent a few sleepless nights praying for God to speak and He did. God told him to love our younger son the way he loves our older son. So when Jeremy asked about the wedding, God said, "Yes. This is one way to love your son the way I intended." There was no question as to what should be done.

However, not everyone thought that way. We were blindsided by the response from the elders of our church. My husband and I had attended our Evangelical church for twenty-five years. He was an elder for many of those years, and we volunteered as much as we possibly could prior to coming on staff. By this time, we had been on staff for ten years as directors of International Ministries. We built a structure around missions that had never existed at our church and we loved our work. Prior to my husband's diagnosis in February 2016, when the elders found out that my husband was going to officiate at our son's wedding, they asked to meet with him to hear his heart about the matter. He met with two of the elders, shared, they thanked him, and we thought that was the end of it.

Six months later, two elders called on the phone to inform us that they decided that they did not want my husband to officiate the wedding because it was inconsistent with what they believed. The wedding was in October, less than two months away. Because we felt that God had spoken about this for our son, and for the sake of the church, we stepped down from our positions. We were shocked and very hurt. This was personal for our family. We shared this with our older son Jamey, and his wife Katie immediately so they could pray for us. We waited to tell Jeremy until the decision to step down was final. We knew he would have tried to prevent the outcome somehow. That is who he is. He loves well.

One of the ironic things about this whole experience was that, Jeremy was a therapist and had provided support and resources to many parents at the church, helping them understand and support their teens. The church's response just didn't make sense.

We created a plan, along with the elders, to step down from our positions, participating in seventeen meetings to share our story with the people that we supported in the field, those in leadership in our ministry, and the others on staff. My husband requested to share our story during a church service but was refused. Nothing was announced, and we left quietly. There are still many people that have no idea why we are gone. There are also those who continue to respect and value our input and contact us often for advice.

We are working through the assault this was to our family. Our older son and his family refuse to go back to the church. They want to raise their children in a place where they are taught to love all people, to love their uncles and not be ashamed. So, the search for a loving and affirming church commenced.

Being persecuted for loving our son was a very painful experience but the persecution that we received was small compared to what the LGBTQ community experiences regularly. As I have come to know many people in the LGBTQ community and have heard their unique stories and of the pain they have endured, I feel compelled to share them with you. Allow your heart to enter each person's life. Get to know them. I am certain that you will love them as I do.

We are thankful for how God has revealed more of His heart through this experience. So, before I share these unforgettable stories, it will be helpful to consider the societal context in which these stories occur.

# *Who do you say I am?*

## Chapter 2

"Who do you say I am?" We answer this question every day by the way we live. We reveal what we believe about God, about ourselves, and about other people. A powerful message is expressed by how we interact with others. Every encounter is an opportunity for us to make a deep, meaningful connection, or to hide behind the fears and prejudices that prevent us from truly getting to know another person.

Our Western culture, particularly the church, has taught us to be blind to the individual by placing people in categories; single, married, divorced, women, men, recovering, disabled, immigrant, and gay. We apply preconceived notions to each group because it helps us to identify who *they* may be. These preconceived notions fail to recognize the value of and embrace the uniqueness of the individual without even hearing their story. Each person's story has the potential to bring a deeper understanding to who they are…and they long to share it. Everyone wants to be known and loved.

Our culture has attempted to respond to this deep desire by providing special opportunities for that to occur. Millions of people, every day, search dating sites for the perfect person. Extensive inventories are completed with the purpose of identifying a compatible partner. The ultimate hope is to find someone who knows and loves them.

But what does it mean to be *known*? Being known requires that we courageously reveal our truest self to another. This willingness to be vulnerable often becomes an invitation for others to respond in kind, creating a beautiful exchange. When we take time to listen to another person, we are communicating that they have value. They have significance. We may not always understand the person but something supernatural happens when we take the time to listen. We communicate love. Listening is the first step to knowing and loving another.

In Psalm 139, David expresses how we are all known by God.

> *You have searched me, Lord and you know me. You know when I sit and when I rise; you perceive my thoughts from afar. You discern my going out and my lying down; you are familiar with all my ways. Before a word is on my tongue you, Lord, know it completely. You hem me in behind and before, and you lay your hand upon me. Such knowledge is too wonderful for me, too lofty for me to attain. (Ps. 139:1-6 NIV)*

David understands what many today fail to realize. Because we are created by God, we are known and loved by Him.

> *For you created my inmost being; you knit me together in my mother's womb. I praise you because I am fearfully and wonderfully*

*made; your works are wonderful, I know that
full well... (Ps. 139:13-14 NIV)*

David concludes this psalm by asking God to look
deep into his heart and reveal those things that are a
hindrance to his spiritual walk. He is completely willing
to receive whatever God desires to share, for the sole
purpose of being known.

*Search me, Oh God, and know my heart; test
me and know my anxious thoughts. See if
there is any offensive way in me, and lead me
in the way everlasting... (Ps. 139:23-24 NIV).*

Jesus was a prime example of vulnerability. He was
God incarnate, entered the world as a tiny baby, born to a
young teenager, in a stable, and lived the life of a human
being so that people on earth could get to know Him. That
is extreme vulnerability.

Being truly known was important to Jesus. He knew
that getting to know someone takes commitment, so He
shared His heart and His life for three years, day-in and
day-out, with an incredibly diverse group of people
because he wanted to develop deep and abiding
relationships with them. Jesus desired for all people to
know His true self and He started with the disciples. Jesus
understood that knowing Him was the first step to loving
Him.

So, in Matthew 16:13-17, After spending much time
with His disciples, Jesus asks them a profound question…
"Who do you say I am?"

*When Jesus came to the region of Caesarea*
*Philippi, he asked His disciples, "Who do*
*people say the Son of Man is?"*
    *They replied, "Some say John the Baptist;*
*others say Elijah; and still others, Jeremiah*
*or one of the prophets."*
    *"But what about you?" he asked. "Who*
*do you say I am?"*
    *Simon Peter answered, "You are the*
*Messiah, the Son of the living God."*
    *Jesus replied, "Blessed are you, Simon*
*son of Jonah, for this was not revealed to you*
*by flesh and blood, but by my Father in*
*heaven.*

Peter's response to Jesus revealed that Peter was really listening…but not just with his ears. Peter was listening with his heart and he was beginning to truly know Jesus.

Getting to know people can be a real challenge. In some church cultures, there is great fear associated with people who are unknown and different. This has prevented many people from being known in the church and has caused them to develop ideas about God that are just plain false. Rules are often established for each group, some spoken…some not. The desire to take a position on a specific issue in the church has often taken precedence over the importance of our posture, how we relate to each other. How are we responding to those who are unknown?

Even taking the first step to knowing and being known by someone else can require much courage. Two years ago, while visiting Seattle with my husband, I remember being overwhelmed with the number of homeless people there and not knowing what to do with my feelings toward this heartbreaking scene. The young people hung together in small communities which was encouraging but the older homeless wandered alone on the streets. As we walked the city, I prayed that God would show me what to do. After walking a while, we ducked into a shopping mall to sit in the atrium, read and sip delicious coffee. I had just been reading the book, *Life Together in Christ*, by Ruth Haley Barton, where she talks about the power of listening to others. Too often in our culture, we believe that adding our "two cents" to someone else's story might possibly be an encouragement to them. The book shared that interjecting one's own experiences into someone else's story has an adverse-affect and causes the person to feel diminished. I was surprised by this and began to really think about how this might affect my future interactions with others.

As I sat and thought about this very powerful message, a homeless woman carrying several bags came and sat near me. She took out her newspaper and began to comment on the articles as if she was broadcasting the news. It was a little unnerving at first and everyone around her paid no attention. She just kept talking very loudly about things that did not make sense. I remember hearing Mao Tse Tung and Winston Churchill mentioned quite a bit during her discourse. She was clearly mentally ill and I did not know what to do about it. Do I pretend that I am not hearing her like everyone else? It just did not feel right to do that, so, I prayed. Then, I heard God speak, "Just look at her." I'm thinking, Lord, I have managed to avoid her gaze in hopes that she would stop. This was a place of vulnerability that I was very reluctant to travel to. And God repeated… "Just look at her." So, I did…right in the eyes. Her gaze was fleeting. She looked around as if there was a veil covering her eyes, but she often looked in my direction as if she knew I was watching. As she continued to talk about things that made absolutely no sense, I smiled and nodded my head as if I understood, praying the entire time, "Oh, Lord, when will she stop?" Then, after about ten minutes of talking, she stopped as abruptly as she started. I was totally undone. I signaled my husband to walk with me so we could debrief this experience, asking what he thought about what just occurred. He had no idea what I was talking about. At first, I thought he was joking. I wept when I realized that this moment was just for me. It was God's response to my prayer. "Help me to know how to respond." "*Just look at her.*"

I will probably never see that woman again, but God was doing something that day as I listened to her. What she shared certainly did not make sense to me but the love of God was being expressed without my saying a word. That happens when we allow ourselves to unselfishly listen to someone. They experience love.

When I speak of love, I am referring to the I Corinthians 13 form of love.

> *If I speak in the tongues of men or of angels, but do not have love, I am only a resounding gong or a clanging cymbal. If I have the gift of prophecy and can fathom all mysteries and all knowledge, and if I have a faith that can*

*move mountains, but do not have love, I am
nothing. If I give all I possess to the poor and
give over my body to hardship that I may
boast, but do not have love, I gain nothing.
Love is patient, love is kind. It does not envy,
it does not boast, it is not proud. It does not
dishonor others, it is not self-seeking, it is not
easily angered, it keeps no records record of
wrongs. Love does not delight in evil but
rejoices with the truth. It always protects,
always trusts, always hopes, always
perseveres. Love never fails. (1Cor. 13:1-8a)*

Jesus disapproved strongly of the self-righteous who
responded to others without love. People so easily passed
judgement on and separated themselves from *others*.
Here is His response to the Pharisee in "The Parable of
the Pharisee and the Tax Collector", in Luke 18:9-14.

*To some who were confident of their own
righteousness and looked down on everyone
else, Jesus told this parable:*

*Two men went up to the temple to pray, one a
Pharisee and the other a tax collector. The
Pharisee stood by himself and prayed: "God,
I thank you that I am not like other people—
robbers, evildoers, adulterers—or even like
this tax collector.*

*I fast twice a week and give a tenth of all I
get."*

*But the tax collector stood at a distance. He
would not even look up to heaven, but beat*

*his breast and said, "God, have mercy on me, a sinner."*

*I tell you that this man, rather than the other, went home justified before God. For all those who exalt themselves will be humbled, and those who humble themselves will be exalted.*

There is a growing intolerance in the world today and the church is one of the primary offenders. Many groups of people have been held at a distance or have been forced to endure immense persecution. This book will address, in part, the vast amount of persecution directed toward the LGBTQ community by the church. Uninformed decisions have been made about this community of people without ever listening to their stories. It is often more of a silent judgement and becomes audible only when the person ventures into a territory where the unspoken rules have been broken.

In some churches, the LGBTQ community is welcome only if they abide by certain "guidelines":

*Thou shall NOT be married in the church.*

*Thou shall NOT have your children dedicated in the church.*

*Thou shall NOT be in any leadership position that has any effect on the church.*

*Thou SHALL come to services, be in a small group, and donate money.*

Having said that, I must add that there are some churches that are very inclusive and invite the LGBTQ community fully into the life of the church. This is the way of Jesus.

It is not an easy path to choose to come out in the Christian community or any other faith community, for that matter. Everything that you hold dear could be sacrificed on the altar of misconceptions; family, friends, and even faith. Many churches today have not even acknowledged a need to examine their response, or lack thereof, to the LGBTQ community. This deafening silence is a rejection that has caused immense hurt and has driven this community and their families from the church.

This became personal for me when my younger son came out, eleven years ago. His story has changed many lives. Through his life, I have had the distinct privilege to meet and get to know many in the LGBTQ community and have been inspired by their courage, and strength. Every one of them desired to be known and loved.

*Who Do You Say I Am?* is a collection of personal life stories told by members of the LGBTQ community. This book is about real people who are created in the image of God and loved by God, that have walked this difficult journey. They are being completely transparent and vulnerable with their stories, sharing their greatest struggles and victories, so that you would know them on a deeper level…and perhaps even love them.

This book is about knowing and loving people. It will not be a theological debate. There are biblical scholars on both sides of this issue for which many books have been written. It is also not to be an extensive criticism of the church. I love the church and believe that the church does many things well. There will, however, be stories about persecution, rejection, forgiveness, redemption, and reconciliation, in which the church has been a part.

This is about a dismantling of the preconceived notions that prevent us from reaching out to those who appear different from ourselves so that we can love well. We do not have to share the same position with someone to love them and treat them with dignity and respect.

Because of the personal nature of these stories, I have changed all names and cities of origin to protect the privacy of each person. Each story was written by me from the information provided by each person during the interviews.

I ask that, as you read this book, you would allow God to open your mind and heart to hear someone's story and be changed. It is my hope that through the power of stories, you would get to know and love individuals and develop a deeper understanding of the LGBTQ community and God's heart for them.

# *John*

## Chapter 3

*Faith was an extremely significant part of John's upbringing. His family attended church every Sunday. He completed all his denominational milestones, was involved in youth group, volunteered with the elderly, and did food drives and other types of community service. This commitment to church continued through his third year of college. It was not until he was a little older that he began to recognize inconsistencies in messages from the church. The messages were hurtful to people. So, when he finally began to accept himself and the same-sex attraction that he had suppressed for so long because of his religion, he began to drift from the church.*

### John's Story

I was raised in the suburbs outside of a large city in the northeast. My family was quite extraordinary. Everything my parents did served to shape my two younger sisters' and my values. They were always very loving and generous people. My mom stayed at home to care for us while my dad provided, working in the same job for many years. They were very supportive, so I always felt safe coming to talk to them about anything. My parents provided a home for us in a neighborhood that was a perfect place to raise a family. My sisters and I spent a great deal of time with our many friends in the neighborhood playing basketball and hockey.

Our very large extended family lived nearby so much of our time was spent with them. It was wonderful growing up with cousins, aunts, and uncles. We celebrated holidays together, vacationed at the beach, even went to church together. This instilled in us a deep sense of family. We are close to this day.

It was in grade school that I first realized I was attracted to the boys in my class and in my neighborhood. I did not understand my feelings at all...but they were real. I just had a connection with the boys that I did not have with the girls. These feelings only intensified through middle and high school but I never shared what I was experiencing with anyone.

I stayed distracted by many activities throughout school. Though I was not very athletic, I tried every sport I possibly could...unsuccessfully. I was an excellent student, however, and was obsessive about my grades and homework. In middle school, I played the clarinet and piano, was in musical theatre, and sang in the chorus. I loved the performing arts. But, all of that stopped when I got to high school. I was afraid that continuing to be involved in those activities would reveal that I was gay. I regret that decision now because I was passionate about music. In high school, I ran track and cross country and was involved in student council.

I only knew of one gay person growing up, my dad's cousin. I'd never met him, and no one ever really talked about him much. Occasionally, I would hear my aunts and uncles joke about him, which made me even more determined to suppress the fact that I was gay.

I also never told anyone I was gay because I had to realize and accept it for myself first. That did not happen until my late teen years. But, even though I knew it I chose to ignore it. For a long time, I attempted to prove to myself that I must be mistaken about my sexual identity. If I just met the right girl, it would change everything. So, in high school, I dated the same girl all the way through but nothing changed.

After I graduated from high school, I went to a very religious college that was founded by my denomination. I went to church every week but the messages that I heard were so judgmental of the gay community that more than ever, I began to question my faith. As I moved closer to accepting my true self, I drifted further from the church that I expected would certainly have passed harsh judgment on my decision.

My attempt to be changed continued in college. I dated two girls. Each time, I hoped that it would transform me but I just could not force it to happen. After I broke up with the second girl, it was apparent that I was gay and was not going to change.

It wasn't until the beginning of my senior year of college, I began to accept the fact that I was gay but I still had not told anyone. The next step was to say the words out loud. "I am gay." I needed to free myself from the secret that I carried for so long. So, at the beginning of senior year, I told a dear friend who seemed like a very safe place for me to start. She was open-minded and had introduced me to several of her gay friends prior to my coming out. Her friends had similar upbringings as me and they seemed happy. It made me realize that living your true self could be fulfilling. Being gay was just one small part of who I was. So, I decided to share my life-long struggle with her. She listened carefully to my story and encouraged me to connect with some of her friends. She was great. A year later, I was out to friends and family.

It was an experience at my college graduation that caused me to cut all ties to the church. President Barack Obama had come to deliver the commencement speech at our college that year. It was quite a unique honor to have the president speak at a graduation. Unfortunately, people from my denomination, students, alumni, and others from the city came to protest his position on abortion. The campus was a circus leading up to the graduation. Obama spoke eloquently addressing the matter directly, speaking about the complexities of abortion and explained that it is not what anyone wants. The protestors were highly offensive, and it caused a major disruption. This was the last straw…I was finished with the church.

I returned home after graduation in 2009 to live with my parents and stayed there for a year and a half. I thought it was probably time to tell my family about my decision to live openly as my true self. I started with my sisters. When I told my two younger sisters, they responded quite differently from one another. The youngest sister thought I was joking with her at first. She was great when she finally realized that this was not some big joke. I was gay. The older of the two immediately became fearful for my parents. She told me that my being gay "might just break up our parents' marriage." She called and apologized a day later telling me how much she loved me.

It was almost Thanksgiving and my dad was traveling for business, so I chose to come out to my mom first. The conversation started with my mom's questions about my dating. When I told her that I probably wouldn't get married, I just couldn't find the right girl, she inquired further asking me why I would say that? Did something happen? She reminded me that I had said that a few times over the last few months and asked if I would explain more. It seemed the perfect time to tell her that I was gay. My mom's reaction was much better than I had anticipated. She was surprised, blamed herself for missing it and felt terrible that I had kept the secret to myself for so long. When my dad returned from his trip I shared my story with him. He cried a lot. Two days later, before leaving on another business trip, my dad shared his heart with me. He hugged me and told me that he would always be my dad. He loved me. My parents did not understand why I had kept it from them for so long. I explained that I was afraid that when I told them, they would kick me out of the house. I had even made plans to move in with a cousin should that happen. They could not believe that I would think they would ever do that. My parents' response to my news was, overall, positive. It did take them a while to adjust their expectations for me. It was helpful that I lived with them for a year after coming out. It gave us all time to adjust to my new life. That was good for all of us as a family. Family is very important to me.

There are many lessons I have learned from my life. Over the last few years, I have met many people from other denominations at weddings and other ceremonies that have caused me to look differently at religion. It is encouraging to know that there are more accepting faiths that embrace the gay community willingly. There are many aspects about my religious upbringing that I cherish and that have been integral to who I am. But the hypocrisy that I have seen has influenced me greatly and I am still trying to determine if I believe in God at all.

I have also learned that as much as you love your family and friends, you must be true to yourself. Part of my struggle in coming out was that I wanted to live up to the expectations of others. But, you cannot live your life for other people. Do not be afraid to speak your mind and express your heart. There will be people who think differently. You do not have to convince them otherwise. There are some people that I realize are unhealthy for me to be around so I steer clear of them and that works for me.

There is no special process on how or when to come out. The timing for coming out is personal. Each person needs to determine what is best for them. I sometimes wonder if I would have come out sooner had I gone to a less religious college. Other classmates of mine came out after graduation. It would have been nice to have had community while we were there.

I know that it is difficult to come out. Every time I share my story, it feels like the very first time. I am still concerned about the reaction I will receive. The interesting thing about that is I have never had a negative reaction. Some people are surprised, but everyone has been caring and supportive to me. I have never lost a friend over my being gay. People who love you will accept you for who you are.

My coming out has exposed me to people with other backgrounds and has helped shape my views. I grew up in a very homogeneous environment. So, after starting my career, when I moved to the city, I was challenged to look at life differently. I am thankful for my partner and the ways he has encouraged me to see through the lens of others. This has opened my eyes to a new world. My goals for the future are no different than they have ever been. Now, a man will be by my side instead of a woman.

*John is a CPA working in a finance-accounting role in a large corporation. He is in a very good place in his career to be thinking about marriage and having a family. Currently, John is living with his partner in the city near his hometown in the northeast.*

# *Jill*

## Chapter 4

*Jill's parents were convinced that she was going to be a boy. Six years had passed between the third and fourth child and her parents believed time may have changed the pattern that they had experienced thus far but it did not. They were quite surprised when she was born their fourth girl. They had not even chosen a name for her beforehand. Jill's father's response was, "Well at least she will play sports." So, she became an athlete.*

### *Jill's Story*

I was always very different from my sisters. They were older when I was born—six, eight, and ten years old. My older sister was charged with babysitting me when my mom went to her part-time job, so I was the closest to her. But most of the time, I was with my dad. So, while I was off with him, my sisters spent time with my mom and became much closer to her.

Dad and I were very close, and he taught me everything he knew about sports and the outdoors. He taught me how to play baseball, basketball, to garden and fish. We were inseparable. I was always with him. I really cherished those moments.

Every evening after dinner, my dad would take me to the local bar and introduce me to his friends. Some of the professional football players gathered at the bar and because my dad was an affluent man and very well known in our area, I got to meet them too.

When it came time for me to play sports, there were no sports teams for girls so I played on the boys' teams. At age eight, a girl playing football was completely unheard of so my mom gave me a boy's name on the application and signed me up for football. I also played on a boys' t-ball team and a "pitch" team—baseball where dads do the pitching.

On Friday nights, our family would go to the fish fry at my aunt and uncle's hotel. My grandfather was a coal miner, so my aunt and uncle ran a hotel in a coal mining town where the miners would stay when they would come to work. My dad's family would gather there on the weekend. It was great fun being with my aunts, uncles, and cousins. My dad was an alcoholic and would sometimes drink too much while we were there which could make it difficult. Much of the time he was functional, but alcohol was a real struggle for him.

I was exposed to a very conservative religion as a child. My dad was insistent that we go to church every Sunday. I was baptized and completed all the milestones required but I really don't know what I thought about it. I was so young. I remember hearing my siblings talk about the discrepancy between who people pretended to be on Sunday, and the way those same people lived their daily lives. It did not match up. My dad would be one person on Sunday and in his career but a totally different person at home with his family. Going to church was something we were supposed to do and that was that.

I was eleven years old when my dad died from complications of alcoholism. My mom packed us up and we moved to the beach. Living at the beach was something we had always talked about, so she decided the time was right. My sisters were grown and out the door by that time so they did not come with us. My mom's response to my dad's death was difficult. It was a type of post-traumatic stress disorder. She had been through so much being married to an alcoholic and spent some time in hibernation after we moved, mostly in her sewing room. She only emerged from that room when she went to grocery shop or go to my sports events. There was nothing more in her life…not even church.

My dad's passion for sports served me well. I became an outstanding athlete. In middle school, I played basketball. It soon became my favorite sport and a force that kept me on the straight and narrow in life. It connected me with a group of people and gave me a purpose.

In high school, I played on the varsity basketball team as a sophomore. I took a little grief from the seniors at first…I got tripped a lot. But, the coach took a strong interest in me. He recognized my athletic talent and was diligent about pushing me to grow into my sport. Even at a height of five feet two inches, I became a very strong point guard. If it wasn't for the team and the encouragement of my coach, I could have gotten into some trouble in high school.

My mom did not have the emotional energy at the time to closely supervise my life, so I had the opportunity to do whatever I wanted. My coach became a surrogate parent that protected me from making unwise decisions.

I chose sports. I also played softball and ran cross country for the track team.

I spent a great deal of time at my best friend's house while in high school. With my mom in solitude, my friend's parents became surrogate parents to me and included me in their family activities. They were highly involved with the "Up with People" movement and brought me along with them. Up with People was an organization whose purpose was to inspire young people to make a difference in their world. They did musical performances to break down cultural barriers and create global understanding. My friend's parents helped with the bands and we sang. For three years, fifteen to twenty students traveled around the state singing with the bands. We even went to the 1984 Olympics to perform. It was a wonderful experience.

Understanding your sexuality is a process. I began to have feelings that I did not understand when I was in tenth grade. I remember being obsessed with the dancer in the movie "Flashdance." I would watch the movie, over and over again. I was fascinated with the dancer but did not know why. It never dawned on me that I might be gay. I dated boys in high school. I always had a boyfriend. It was not until I got to college that I began to understand my sexuality.

I always wondered if my dad's influence of sports in my life caused me to be who I am today, but my family has shared stories that suggest additional influences. My sisters told me that when I was young, people would ask if I was their little brother. I wore my hair short, and I never liked to wear my shirt. I wore Spiderman and cowboys' outfits. I was drawn to GI Joes, never played with dolls, and I would rather play tag outside than play kitchen. I was more interested in running, jumping, climbing, and getting dirty, and I grew up in a family of girls. They were not interested in the same things. Now, that was *not* my dad's influence. I chose those things that I most wanted to do. We thought nothing of it at the time.

When I graduated from high school and went on to college, I had my first exposure to gays and lesbians that were my age. I had a good friend who was a lesbian on my softball team. She introduced me to her friends who were gay. People never talked about their sexuality at that time, you just knew. In college, I started dating women sophomore year.

We never talked about my sexuality in my family until many years later. I think my dad would have really had a hard time accepting it. He probably would have flipped out. My mom had a very hard time with it. I told her my second year of college. She had had a sense about it but never mentioned it or understood this fully. After I graduated from college, I moved south with a person I was dating at the time and we lived together for four years. Mom shared her concern and disapproval of my lifestyle with my sisters.

I did have three relatives on my dad's side that were gay but no one ever talked about it. I had a cousin on my dad's side, my cousin's oldest daughter, and an uncle that were gay. So, if there is anything to genetics, the gay gene came from my dad's side.

My cousin lived her secret life until she was in her thirties. She never shared with her parents about her lifestyle because she knew they would highly object. I remember going to spend the night with my aunt as a child. In her hallway was a shrine of a religious figure illuminated twenty-four hours a day, seven days a week, to remind them of their religion. It was so ingrained in our thinking that my cousin was not allowed to be herself. She was not allowed to be gay because of her religion. She later married a man. They have no children. She says she is happy, but I know her other life and I wonder about that.

My cousin couldn't be open with her mom but I could be with my aunt (her mom). When I opened up to my aunt about my sexuality, she did not really accept or challenge me, she just listened. Yet, she never would have accepted her daughter.

I met my wife in 1994 while I was living at the beach. We met at a party with mutual college friends and stayed friends for a few years. We would go biking or to the beach together. We did not start dating until after my mother died in 1996.

We were married in a ceremony in 2000 before gay marriage was legal. November 2016, we finally had an actual wedding ceremony. We invited our family to celebrate with us. I invited my aunt and cousins but a week before the ceremony, one of my sisters discouraged my aunt out from attending. Only one of my three sisters came to our wedding. My oldest sister and I had been very close because she was the one who would babysit me but she refused to come. This was very hurtful because her life has been a mess. As much as she took care of me when I was little, I have taken care of her as an adult— health-wise, emotionally, and financially. My sister that is closest to my age, got involved in a religious group and is outwardly opposed to the gay lifestyle. She sent a scathing five-page letter that was very hurtful telling me that I was going to burn in hell and so would my children. She was the one that talked behind my back to all my family members which caused my aunt to choose not to come to the wedding. This response put a wedge between us. I believe my sister's heart has started to soften by her interactions with me but her beliefs have not changed. I am not emotionally comfortable with any of my sisters right now, nor do I care to have a relationship with them. None of them know what goes on in my life. My wife loves one of my sisters and tolerates the others.

We have three children: a fourteen-year-old son, twelve-year-old son, and nine-year-old daughter. My wife gave birth to all three after a few years of infertility. Giving birth was not something I volunteered to do. They are amazing children.

Our friendships have changed through the years since we started having children. We used to have many gay friends but most of them were not having children. As our focus on our family became the priority, our gay friendships began to change. We started to have more in common with our heterosexual friends with families and that has become our community. I think we are the straightest gay couple I know. We do see our gay older friends on occasion.

Through the years, I have had some ambivalence about religion because of my experience. Since I came out, I have been guarded. I kind of put church in the same category as my sisters…two steps removed. It is important to me to learn from the Bible so I listen to the audio Bible daily. I did return to church when we started to have children because my wife believed that it was important for them. She believed that the religious community would embrace us.

Sadly, much of the most hurtful persecution we have received has been through the church. We went to one church that called us into a meeting to inform us that we could not be members of their church. We could attend, but we could not be members or serve in any capacity. When we questioned them about this, they said that we were living in sin as a gay couple. My wife really struggled with that but I was not at all surprised. I wonder how persecution is consistent with Christian values.

We were not defeated by this response, we changed churches. Though the people at our current church seem welcoming, I feel we are held at a distance. Our boys have been volunteering in the children's ministry and our house church is very open and affirming. I have also heard that the new pastor would like to address the LGBTQ issue in the church in the future. There is no overt discrimination, but we are not 100 percent welcome either. Sadly, I really did not expect to be. Experiences like we have had are what deters the LGBTQ community from coming to church.

Our children have also received persecution in school. In late elementary and middle school, our oldest son was teased about having two moms. Not as much has happened since he is in high school. Our younger son has also received comments, but he is not as vocal about it. Our daughter is still young enough that she has been protected from that.

Today, many people in the gay community believe that there is no room for being a Christian and being gay, that you must make a choice between the two. Don't buy into that belief. You do not need to choose between a loving God and being gay. Growing up, I could not do both and it moved me away from God and the church. It does not have to be mutually exclusive. You do need to understand that there will be people that will not accept you. Don't let that take away from your identity or take you away from your faith.

*Jill is a social worker and licensed therapist in practice with her wife. She no longer plays basketball but is a die-hard fan of women's basketball. Jill is happily married living with her wife and three children in the northeast.*

# Elliott

## Chapter 5

*Elliott's parents were married during the Vietnam war. His dad had enlisted in the Navy after graduating from college and went to OCS. It wasn't long after that his parents found themselves on a US military base overseas. Because he was an engineer, Elliott's dad was assigned to the Seabees (C.B.): the US Naval construction forces. Elliott was conceived while they were overseas and when his dad was sent to Vietnam, his mother went back to their hometown to give birth to him.*

### Elliott's Story

I was six months old when I met my dad for the first time. I was told that he was happier to see the cats than to see me. I guess that has been a theme in my life…feeling like other things take precedence over me.

My being an only child made it easier for my parents to focus on their careers. After my dad's time in the service, my parents became business partners. My mother was an interior designer and my dad an engineer. I remember that they were always working. I never doubted that they loved me, but their focus was always work or each other. I spent most of my time with a lovely housekeeper who cared for me most every day.

There was quite a dichotomy between my parents' cultural backgrounds. They were from totally different social classes. I say that because this was very important in our family.

My dad came from a small town 30 miles away from where we lived. My paternal grandfather was a blue-collar worker in a chemical plant. I am not sure he ever graduated from high school. He was down to earth and kind. My paternal grandmother was a good influence in that she was very nurturing. She taught me compassion. They were not into high society...more down home. Because they endured the depression era, they were more concerned about eating and much less concerned about the school you were attending. The fact that my dad graduated from college made his parents very proud.

My mother was raised in a very affluent family. Her dad was an oil man. When he died, she and her brother inherited some family money. This allowed for a very comfortable lifestyle. It was helpful to have money, but it did not meet the needs of every issue. My maternal grandmother struggled with depression and when the burden of it became too much, she took her own life. She had heart problems so when I was a child, I was told that she had a heart attack. The true story was, in 1968, my grandmother went to the beach, took all her pills and died in the car. I did not know about this until I was much older. I am certain that the memory of this runs through my mother's mind even today. This experience created an unresolved psychological issue in my family.

Societal appearances were important to my mother's family. Even the Episcopal church that my mom attended while growing up was for the high society type. It was more of a cultural thing to do.

Unlike his parents, my dad did like the high society life. Moving to the big city was great for him. This caused a little friction between he and my grandfather at times. My grandfather just did not understand "fancy living." As a child, I was protected from whatever issues that they had.

So, my mom inherited the money, made the money, and made all the decisions, personal and business. She was the boss and still is. They are now seventy-four and seventy-six and have been married for fifty years.

I attended a private elementary school. Schooling brought some social challenges at an early age, however. I was teased for being different. As an only child with working parents, I was starved for attention. At age six and seven, I found joy in chasing the boys and girls to kiss them at school. No one ever told me this was not right. I was labeled "gay" even before children at this age understood the meaning. I denied it of course. This was not a positive way to grow up.

When I was young, I was not really into sports. I attempted to play soccer and basketball but was not very coordinated, so my parents didn't push it. It helped that my dad was not very athletic. Fortunately, when I was older, I discovered that I enjoyed solitary sports like running and weight lifting. This would have been beneficial at an earlier age.

Our financial position allowed for us to travel frequently. We traveled to Europe several times so my mom could select antiques for her clients—London,

Paris, French countryside. I have very fond memories of this time with them, from sixth grade through high school. When the oil bust occurred in 1986, the flow of cash stopped and so did the trips, but we always had enough and lived in a nice home.

Despite my parents' church background, faith was never big in our family. We were Episcopal and my parents made sure that I received a religious education. They would drop me off at church once a month to serve as an acolyte. When I was old enough, I drove myself to church.

Because my mother is a very strong woman, she has had the greatest influence on me. Unfortunately, it was probably not all in a positive way. She would quote things her mother would say that were contradictory to what she herself modeled for me. "My mother says that you should be nice to everyone." Yet, she herself was not always nice or kind. She was very class conscious and prejudiced and talked about my friends in that way. For example, she would say, "She is not really in your class." And though she wanted me to be successful in school, she did not always support me in the best way. She would tell me, "You better make good grades," and then she would bribe me in fourth, fifth, and sixth grade with money.

Sex was never a topic of discussion in my family. I never heard about sex between a man and a woman from my parents. I heard that from a friend when I was in third grade.

Being gay was very secretive during this time so there were very few people I could talk about the same-sex attraction that I was experiencing. I did have a close girlfriend from middle school whose family was very accepting. The mom was "cool" and extremely liberal. She smoked pot...very different from my mother. Elsa was someone that I "came out" to later, along with my girlfriends in my senior year of high school.

When I was a teenager, I started to experiment with sex. My attraction to the same sex was confirmed. Initially, I tried to fight it. Then I started to look at magazines and liked the ones that had men in them more than the women.

I had my first boyfriend in high school. We were only together for three months. I wanted to break up with him because he was very feminine...more queen like...flamboyant. I was uncomfortable with that and not attracted to him.

Once sexually active, I would look for guys in the community. There were no gay guys my age that were out, so I began to experiment with older men. Living as a gay teenager was dangerous, during this time. You really had to search for people. There was no easy way to make a connection with people that were gay, not at safe places like church, community centers, leagues, civic organizations, or the internet. So, I found myself going to unsafe places like bars, parks, and bathrooms. These proved to be all the wrong places. I went to my first gay bar when I was eighteen.

In 1988, my life was changed when I was robbed at knifepoint after a random "encounter." I had been cruising around town looking for someone with one purpose in mind. I met this guy who seemed decent. After our encounter, he told me to give him all my money or he would kill me. I jumped out of the moving car that we were traveling in and ran to my car. This alarmed him and he drove away.

This put into motion my coming out to my parents. Shaken, I told a good friend about this experience at 3:00 am and she advised that I tell my mother that night. So, I did. The next afternoon my parents took me to a psychiatrist because they thought I needed therapy and medication to treat the trauma. I went once a week for a few months and then the visits ended. I got over the traumatic experience and could function in life. There was really nothing wrong with me so the doctor never did prescribe medication. After our visits, the doctor said there was nothing more to discuss.

My mom's response to my coming out was typical. She told me that this was probably a "phase" I was going through. "This was a lifestyle." She told me, "This was not an easy lifestyle." As if I had a choice? She asked, "Do you want to pick the easy life or this difficult lifestyle?" Why would I choose a more difficult lifestyle? Why would I choose prejudice, judgment, and discrimination? It was who I was, not a choice. We did not really talk about it after that. The topic went underground. "Don't ask don't tell."

In the eighties, there were no positive role models for gays anywhere. Gay characters on television were portrayed in a negative manner, at the time; hairdressers, flaming, flamboyant queens, and flight attendants, etc. There is nothing wrong with these people but they were all extreme. There were never traditional gay people living in society or traditional activities seen. As a teenager, there were no proms for gays. The television show "Will and Grace" came out later but it was not until 1998. Everyone was more closeted.

I went to Davidson for my first year of college then transferred and graduated from Emory with a degree in Political Science. This was an era when people became aware of AIDS…so that stopped a lot of sexual behavior. The headlines, "Rock Hudson has AIDS," caused people to be more cautious. There was no treatment for AIDS then and this was sobering.

People started practicing safer sex as a result. Treatment did not come around until 1996 which made AIDS a more manageable disease.

In the mid-nineties, gay people tried to fight against the stigma of being gay and many started to come out. People became more emboldened to not be hidden. They wanted to get educated to fight AIDS. It helped that the media became more informative about the disease. The internet has been very helpful today.

My college years soon became the happiest extended time in my life. In 1992, I was accepted as an intern at the White House. George Bush was president at the time. I was never really a Republican but did vote for him in 1988. I was shocked that I got the job. I took a leave of absence from Emory and for four months I worked in Washington, DC. I lived in an apartment in Pentagon City, Arlington. It was the most enjoyable experience of my life. I met so many people. I went out every night. The highlight was visiting the Oval Office twice. It was captivating. It is amazing to think that the people in history books were all in that room. It was an intoxicating experience.

Life went downhill from there. When your life peaks at age twenty-one, it is extremely difficult. By the time I graduated from college, the administration had changed in Washington, DC. Clinton was in office and even though I voted for Clinton and liked the Democrats, all the people I knew in the White House were gone because of the party change.

I met my first partner in 1995 at age twenty-five. We met in a bar. When I moved to a large southern city to do retail, he followed. He was a car dealer. He was six years older, larger and heterosexual-looking. That is probably why I was attracted to him. I found that when I was with someone, it was easier to tell my parents about my life. My partner was my ally. If my mom would have had a daughter, she would have wanted that kind of person for her son-in-law. He seemed very straight. He went to LSU, was a fraternity guy and he made a lot of money. We lived together for a while then adopted a baby together. The day our son was born was one of the most amazing days of my life. His birth mother was very young and smoked pot when she was pregnant. He was born blind in his right eye. My partner and I were together twelve years.

My second partner was married and living at home with a wife and three daughters when I first met him. He got separated, came out of the closet and eventually got divorced. He was always worried about what his daughters would think of him. He also wondered, "What would society think? What would his business partners think?" He realized that they may think about it or mention it for a while and then go back to their own lives. It took four years for him to get divorced. Our relationship ended shortly thereafter. We were together just shy of five years.

After I split up from my second partner, I decided that I wanted to meet someone in a larger, more liberal northern city. People asked, "Why would you go to a large northern city when your son lives in a southern city?" It's difficult to explain. I love my son, but I never liked the large southern city and I never wanted to be there. This was a theme that goes back to childhood. I always wanted to be somewhere else. "Then, I'll be happy," I thought. This doesn't always come true but sometimes it stays in your head forever—the idea of a geographical cure.

People say the third time's the charm…right? Well, my third partner was not my "lucky number." It was the lowest point in my life. I found him on a dating site. He was a lawyer and thirteen years older than me. I liked older men. Like a moron, I met him and one month later, we signed an apartment lease. Don't sign a lease with someone you just met!

I found out later that he was a very jealous man. One day, when we were at the gym, he watched me and asked, "What are you doing? Are you trying to show off?" This became a theme in our relationship. He really didn't want me to exercise. He believed that it drew attention to me. It was really an odd thing and in time, escalated into a point of violence.

He was an alcoholic and lost his job two months after we moved downtown. I became this man's "babysitter."

The bank didn't leave him destitute…he had some money, so I didn't support him financially. I would not leave him because I felt bad for him. I've always been a people-pleaser.

This brings up another theme that has run through my life. I thought I needed to find someone that could pay for everything. I learned later that you should seek to support yourself. Don't rely on others to do that. You do not want to become someone's employee or slave. That can happen. People get into a situation where they cannot afford their own life. It was terrible.

The relationship between my partner and I became increasingly violent. When I would exercise or smoke, he would "freak." I am not just talking about yelling. He would become violent. If I would fight back, he would call the police on me.

The first time this happened, I left. When I explained that I wanted to exercise, he freaked out so I grabbed my dog and went to a hotel. I stayed there one night, then rented a car that cost a thousand dollars and drove south. For three nights, I dodged a snowstorm. I returned a short time later.

Once you get into a cycle of violence with someone, it is difficult to get out of it. When someone is abused…the easy response from people is to say, "Just leave. Why would you put up with that?" But wait until you are in it. Then you ask, "But where would I go? Am I going to go back home in my mid-forties and live with my parents?" They would have taken me back but I didn't want to do that. I don't know whether it was pride, or what.

Eventually, we moved south together because he thought it would be easier to get a job there, but it wasn't. He started drinking more and more, from morning until he went to bed. He was at the level of alcoholism that he didn't want to go restaurants if didn't serve alcohol. If we did, he would pour coke out of the can and fill it with wine. Then, he would take it with him into restaurants. Or...he would fill a water bottle with vodka and walk around with it. People would never know.

I was a flight attendant and one of the benefits was that spouses can travel at a reduced rate. We were married so that he could have the airline benefit to visit his ninety-year-old mother back in the north.

The relationship continued to be abusive. My partner continued to call the police when we didn't agree. I took photos of the battering that I received every time. I left so many times because of violence that I earned a free night in the hotel where I stayed. I knew that I was going to leave him eventually, but I continued to go back. This is the cycle of violence.

One night, I was working a flight to a large city and my partner accompanied me. We went to the bar in the hotel and he abruptly took my phone out of my hand and said he was not giving it back. He proceeded to run out the door and I followed. He ran into a bathroom and tried to throw my phone in the toilet. Someone must have reported the incident because the hotel security arrived and questioned us. Here we were staying in a hotel paid for by my company. When security asked if we wanted them to call the police, my partner, who was very inebriated answered, "Yes...call the police. I want to call the police because he is trying to attack me." He could never solve a domestic situation without calling the police. I would never call the police. Since we were married, they decided to take us both down to the precinct. We were put in jail for assault for twenty hours. Separate cells. I had to call work to say I was unable to take my scheduled flight. I didn't want to call in sick because they will fire you for that. There was a payphone at the jail, eight-hundred numbers work at a payphone, so I called to say I wasn't coming.

I was released from jail at 8:00 pm that night. I went to collect my things from the hotel and checked into another hotel. I knew when lying on the jail cell floor that I could be fired. I was arrested on a layover. I had been employed with them for thirteen years.

I went back home the next day. The airline was concerned and wanted to know what happened. I was put on a leave of absence for two weeks…paid leave. Then, they started to investigate me. Two times I went in to tell my story. My union representative went with me. I was interrogated then they called me back a second time because they didn't think that I was forthright with my answers. If I hadn't been covered by the union, I think I would have been fired. I didn't lose my job. I got suspended for six days.

That was the end of the relationship. My partner almost cost me my job. The worst thing in my life was meeting him and being in a relationship with an alcoholic. I knew, when I was lying on the floor of the jail, that if I did not leave him, I was going to die. Or, I was going to kill him and be in prison for the rest of my life. The court put orders of protection in place for both of us for six months. We had to return three weeks after the incident for a hearing. The court said that if nothing else happened this incident would be removed from our records. That was the last time I ever saw him. A legal divorce followed. It was no contest. We each took our own things and split the legal fees.

My ex-partner is now working in a large US bank as a senior vice president. How someone can drink at that much and function in a high level executive position in a major bank is a mystery. Maybe he got help. I don't know. He wouldn't get help when we were together. Dealing with someone with addiction is difficult.

I have experienced depression off and on in my life. Suicide was never an option for me because of my maternal grandmother's exit from this world. Sometimes I have thought about how I don't want to do this life anymore. As an adult, when I am hungry, angry, lonely, tired, I can feel that way. Usually, if I fix one of those, I don't feel that way anymore. Living with an alcoholic did lead me to a support group. Exposure to the *Twelve Steps* helped me to deal with all the trauma I had endured. I return to this group now and then for the support. I also find that I receive much comfort and support from listening to Joel Osteen's podcasts.

My parents have had a difficult time watching my life choices. Over the last few years, I have had some disagreements with my dad, never about the gay topic, but he always wants to be right about everything. If you correct him, he gets angry. This could be related to his relationship with my mother. Also, the experience with my third partner was traumatic. My parents never wanted me to get married again after that.

I think that I have gone counter to what I learned growing-up. I am more inclusive and not elitist or snobby. I'm not really interested in society. At times, I do find Vanity Fair interesting or read about rich and wealthy people but more out of curiosity than anything else.

My advice to other gays is don't be afraid to be who you are. Don't worry about what others think about you. It's been my experience that people aren't thinking about you as much as you think they are. People can be selfish and egocentric for the most part and usually worry more about what is going on in their own lives. You can't control what others think about you or how they will react to you. Surround yourself with a group of people that is accepting of you and don't worry about those that reject you. If people don't like it…well…sorry.

I am lucky to have the job that I do. Though, I do complain about it at times. As a flight attendant, it is difficult to be away from your family so much. If I want to make money…I need to travel. But, I can support myself. Take my advice, don't rely on others to support you. Do whatever you can to be self-sufficient. It's not always easy but you can do it.

I felt trapped by my first three partners. A relationship with someone should complement your life…and make life more fulfilling.

*Elliott is happily married to Luca and living in the south where he continues to work as a flight attendant.*

## Elliott

*He has discovered a love for acting and musical theatre and has been attending classes when he can.*

# Ruth

## Chapter 6

*Ruth was fortunate to have very a supportive family and friends that loved and accepted her unconditionally. So, her story is a little different than that of many LGBTQ people coming out. Ruth's family never used their faith in God to pass judgement on her. They were a clear reflection of what love looks like. For that, she is truly grateful.*

### Ruth's Story

I come from a long line of very strong women. My grandmother played basketball in college, was very active in her church, and became a teacher. My mother was a single parent raising two girls, has a Master's in Theatre, and worked for the post office for over thirty years. Both are amazing women who taught me right from wrong and supported me throughout my life. Because of them, I am the woman I am today.

My grandfather was the father figure in my life. My parents divorced before my younger sister was born. She is twenty months younger than me. I was so young that I have no memory of our father. My grandfather was always there for us. He was a college professor and taught statistics nearby.

You would think that because my sister and I were so close in age we would have similar interests, but we could not have been more different. I was the big sister. I spent my time reading books and playing sports. I was always considered the strong one. I never got into trouble because I followed all the rules. She was the complete opposite. We were not very close growing up because of our differences but that changed as we got older. She is married now with an adorable son and lives in our hometown in the south.

So, our family consisted of my mother, little sister, and grandparents. I was very close with my grandmother, and my sister to my grandfather.

My spiritual upbringing was rather diverse. I went to a Church of the Brethren church with my grandparents on Sundays if I got myself ready and in the car before they left. It was much like the Mennonite church and was very focused on serving others. It was always my choice to go. Church was very important to me as it was some of the best times that I had growing up—lots of friends, lots of food, and lots of love. I was also exposed to other faiths by my mother. She is a spiritual person, so we would discuss other faiths and beliefs.

I began to show interest in the same sex when I was seven years old but honestly, I don't remember a time when I wasn't aware of liking women. What I do remember is the moment when I realized that it might not be acceptable to like women. I was seven-years-old, and my sisters and I were playing with our Barbie dolls. We had a large dollhouse and at "bedtime," I wanted Barbie and Barbie to sleep together. My little sister said, "That's not how it works. Barbie and Ken sleep together." From that moment on, I became worried that there might be something wrong with me because I just couldn't understand why Barbie would want to sleep with Ken. So, I spent the next few years not saying anything about it and praying that God would fix whatever was wrong with me.

The first time I had a crush on someone it wasn't someone I knew, it was on the actress Christina Ricci. I had seen her in *Casper* and *Now & Then*. She just seemed so cool to me. I hung her pictures around my room, just like my sister did of famous boy actors. But I never said a word about it being a crush.

We had a babysitter, Jodi, who my sister and I adored. I would not describe my feelings for her as a crush, but I admired her and wanted to marry someone just like her when I grew up.

So, from age seven to fourteen, believing that what I was experiencing was wrong, I spent a great deal of time praying for God to right the wrong in me.

During that time, I was very involved in my church and cultivating a spiritual life, a Christian life that was based around service to others. I never heard a word about gay people in church and I did not ask. From this time of praying, serving, and worshipping, I came to realize that God truly loves me. He loves everything about me because He made me> Once I realized that, I did not care what anyone else thought of me because they were not my Creator.

Some of my happiest memories were made at our church camp, Camp Bethel. Camp Bethel was a church camp that was founded by my great grandfather. Our entire family attended the camp at some time. I looked forward to going there every year. I loved everything about it—the hymns, the hiking, the friends, and "Vesper Hill." Vesper Hill was a special place at the foot of the Blue Ridge Mountains where you could go to see the sunrise and sunset. I made some lifelong friends going to that camp. Every year my same group of friends would come to spend time together. As I got older, I helped with the vacation bible school there. I loved working with the children. There was also a group of summer staff that came from Poland each year. They were older than I but I always felt more comfortable around older people. We became close friends and are still friends to this day.

Some of my fondest memories were in Belize. My uncle had a house there as did my mother's best friend. It was great for my mom to be able to do what she loved, scuba dive. My favorite trip was when my grandmother went. I can still picture her in her Hawaiian shirt and shorts. It makes me laugh.

It was not until I entered middle school, that I started hearing jokes or comments about same-sex attraction. They were not directed toward me...I was not out yet.

When I was fourteen years old, I confided in my cousin about the same-sex attraction that I was experiencing. I think I told her because I had a crush on her. She responded by telling me that I needed to get out of the small southern town I was in and move to a more progressive city. She was worried that people would not accept me in a small town. My relationship with my cousin became even stronger after sharing with her and today she is the person in my family to which I am the closest.

I came out to my mom two weeks later. She and I were going to rent a movie. We were driving down the back roads and I just came out with it. I was worried about telling her. My mom was really great. She told me that she already knew.

I had many interests growing up—reading, softball, and the Spice Girls. I spent a great deal of time alone reading but when I got to high school, I played softball and was in the marching band's color guard.

One of the saddest times in my life was when two of my friends died. It was sophomore year, I had been friends with Sean since fifth or sixth grade. He lived down the street with his parents and twin sisters. He was cleaning a gun and it went off right into his stomach. There were questions as to whether it was intentional or not. Then, two weeks later, my friend from camp died in a car accident. It was a very difficult time for me.

When I was in high school, I had a crush on one of my good friends. We would hang out all the time and spend hours talking on the phone. But, I always knew it was not reciprocated because all she did was talk about boys. I wasn't really worried about it though because I always believed that "when I get to college or when I moved out of our small town," I would find people like me. The special person that God has out there for me will show up when the time is right. I can't say that my feelings toward this good friend made any difference in our relationship because I never voiced them. What did change our friendship was when I came out.

I did make some close friends that were gay in high school. We hung out all the time. My shaved head and boy's clothes helped inform others of my sexuality. This was when people started to make comments toward me.

I came out to my grandparents because I was at a pride parade and happened to be interviewed by the paper, *The Times*. They wanted to know what it was like to be "out." They used my name in the article, so I made the decision to tell my grandparents before they saw the paper. My youth pastor already knew about me, so I gathered my grandparents, the youth pastor, and pastor together to inform everyone at the same time. The youth pastor was very supportive! The pastor and my grandfather said they needed to study scripture more closely about this issue. We never talked about it again. My grandparents were very accepting when I would bring a girlfriend around. My grandmother would ask, "Is this a girlfriend-girlfriend or a girlfriend?" They were great.

My sister was the last person that I told I was gay...my junior year. I was afraid to tell her because she had made a comment many years before that if I was gay, she would disown me. She supports me now and denies ever saying that.

My family has been very accepting of me coming out. No one else in my family is gay but we have a very close friend who is. My mom's best friend didn't come out until after I did. In fact, he told me that my coming out helped him to do the same.

I thought I would grow up to be a pastor like so many of the people on my grandmother's side of the family had been. When it came time for me to make that decision there were many factors that stood in my way. I was a gay woman and needed to know what that meant for my life. I couldn't lead others in a church if I was still figuring out who I was. So, I made the decision not to go into ministry.

After high school, I took some classes at the community college in town, but I got my real college experience hanging out with students from the dance and art departments at a college nearby. The professors loved that I had a sincere interest in learning and allowed me to sit in on their classes. I wanted to go to college but the cost was prohibitive at the time.

I have had two serious relationships in my life. The first time was when I was living in Baltimore and in my early twenties. We were together for a few years. She was older, set in her ways, and very emotionally abusive. When it ended, I was devastated even though I had wanted it to end. As I look back on our relationship, I realize that the way she treated me had nothing to do with me but more with her inability to reconcile her sexuality. We remain friends.

The second relationship was just in the last few years. I fell for her the first night we met. The relationship became quickly passionate and emotional. I thought that I had found the one, that we would spend our lives together. But we were in two different places in life and she ended it. I was crushed, and I didn't think my heart would ever recover. But with the help of my faith, yoga, and a good therapist, my heart has healed.

The most important lesson that I have learned is that love is the most important thing in life. I must love myself first and foremost, then I am capable of loving others as well.

Everyone needs to make their own decision as to when the right time is to come out. You need to do it when you are ready. It is probably the scariest thing I have ever done but I can promise you will feel better about yourself once you do… regardless of the reactions you get.

My life is different than I thought it would be. I believed that I would be married, with children and a house by now. My hope is that I would continue to learn, explore, evolve, and most of all, be happy in everything that I do.

*Ruth is currently working as a restaurant manager out west and is thinking about becoming a certified yoga instructor*

# Eric

## Chapter 7

*Attending an exclusive all-male private high school was a very difficult transition from the public school Eric had attended in prior years, for so many reasons. He was gay and resented the hyper-masculine, heteronormative culture that focused on being exceptional at sports. Eric appeared to fit the model there because he enjoyed being athletic, and "passed" as the image of an athlete but he didn't see it as his sole interest. The teachers were encouraging so Eric found himself gravitating to them. They were easier to relate to.*

### Eric's Story

I only knew of one other gay person at my school…my best friend. We were very close. I went on many trips with his family and we became a couple for a few months. He courageously came out senior year at a ceremony held for the parents. Students were given an opportunity to share…and he publicly shared about his sexuality. Most people were shocked.

His coming out caused some contention between me and my parents. They had many questions. After the ceremony, while we were driving home, my mom confronted me on the subject.

"Why didn't you tell me that your best friend was gay?" she asked.

I responded, "Well, it really wasn't any of your business and it's not really a big deal," since I knew they would not be comfortable with it.

She must have suspected something about me because she continued. "If you are gay, I will still love you." I was not comfortable with the way the conversation was going so I did not engage. I had not become fully comfortable with it myself. I knew my parents would not approve.

Two hours later, my mom returned to the same conversation. She clearly was upset. "If you are gay, it is okay but it's wrong." Then she proceeded to quote the Bible passages that have been believed to be about homosexuality to me.

"No and you are being crazy." I avoided the topic completely.

My dad responded in my defense, "Just give the kid a break already." That was the end of the conversation.

Most of my personal growth, at this age, took place while abroad. My love and passion for travel, different cultures, and animals took me to South Africa for six weeks when I was in eleventh grade. I volunteered at a rehabilitation clinic for injured penguins and other seabirds.

My experience working at the local zoo made me believe that I might enjoy being a veterinarian, so I was excited about the opportunity to go abroad to work with animals. It was also a great opportunity to leave high school behind. My parents also thought that this experience would look good on my college applications.

I went to Ecuador, during the gap year following graduation. I wanted an experience where I could recreate myself…come out of my shell. I was also unsure of what I wanted to study in college and wanted to make the most of my classes. I believed that taking a year off would help me learn not only about myself, but about my interests as well. I wanted to grow as a person in a challenging environment. I was drawn towards the opportunity of being able to learn another language. I went with a group of students from the United States who had just graduated from college. We all lived with indigenous host families. They were so encouraging to me that I felt like I could be myself, so I shared my true identity with them. They were amazing.

Persecution became very real for me on that trip, however. Some of the locals overheard me sharing with my friends about my sexual orientation, and before I knew it, I was being beaten up. One of my friends had mentioned that I was gay to one of the men she had met from the capital. She, being an extremely open-minded woman, thought nothing of it, especially after one of the boys shared that he was "bi." I don't know if it was true or not. A group of boys that my friend had met decided to visit the area we were living in the jungle region. They were around the same age as our team, eighteen to twenty years of age. Without warning, the group of boys jumped me as I was walking to meet my host aunt at a local bar. My aunt saw what was happening and chased the boys away not long after it started. Later, the local townspeople had heard what had happened and stood up for me. The boys ended up receiving a beating of their own and were told to leave town. Fortunately, I did not sustain any serious injuries. I have been very careful in the way I present myself to people since then.

Overall, the opportunities to go abroad helped me to feel more secure about who I am and are what gave me the courage to face one of my biggest fears…telling my family. All my friends, outside of high school, already knew that I was gay at this point. They had been very encouraging to me. It was family that needed to be informed. In preparation for the "outing," I talked to my aunt, my mom's sister, first. She believed that my mom would be fine. My mom had also talked to my aunt because she was wondering if I was gay. She expected, "It wouldn't be that big of an issue." I knew that it would not be that simple.

My coming out did not go over well with my parents. In the span of an hour, I told my entire family. I spoke to my mom first.

Mom was alone in the basement working out. I thought it was the perfect time to share with her what I had been experiencing for many years. The conversation started with a discussion about a girl I had met in Ecuador from my team. I had really wanted to fall in love with her but did not. I explained to my mom that my relationship with the girl "was just not going to happen. I don't like girls like that."

"So, you don't like girls at all?" Later, she asked if I would ever consider being with a girl in the future. She was worried about my eternal soul. I told her I would be open to the possibility, mainly to get to her stop but that I couldn't ever see it happening.

Then, I prepared my brother before I talked to my dad so he could be braced for the fallout—weird tension in the house. He was great.

He just said, "Yeah, I've known. It's fine."

When I told my dad, he uttered a partial sentence, "I have to go... dog... walk... garage." He left the house with the dog, went for a long walk and I did not see him for the rest of the night. We have not talked about it much since. I try to avoid bringing the topic up because it is obvious my dad doesn't know how to approach it, and it makes him uncomfortable. On numerous occasions, my dad has made comments about how I dress—normally when I wear pants that are tight, i.e. skinny jeans, etc. I can tell it embarrasses him and I think it's because people may think that I am gay, even though I don't always project the stereotypical "image" of a gay man. There have been times where my father has made homophobic comments, mostly in scenarios where it doesn't even make sense. I remember one time we were watching television and the news was detailing President Obama's workouts. Keep in mind that my father is a staunch republican, listens to Rush Limbaugh, and watched Bill O'Reilly almost religiously. He also owns several of his books. On the news, he saw how Obama was working out and laughed out, "What a faggot." I gave him a surprised look after that and wasn't even sure how to respond.

I never came out with the words, "I am gay." I just did not feel comfortable at the time, but they totally understood what I was implying. Even now, bringing it up is still an awkward topic.

My brother was great when I came out. I have always had a very close friend in him. He is two years younger than me and much more outgoing so it always felt like we were the same age. We did everything together. Most of my fondest memories have him in them.

We felt like a normal family growing up. We lived in the perfect neighborhood… many kids. My best friend, Susie, lived next door. We would spend countless hours outside with the other neighborhood kids climbing trees, playing tag and other imaginary games. We all went to the public school together.

In the winter, after a day out in the snow, my brother and I would hang out by the wood furnace in the basement. We would build forts and the dogs would join in with the fun. I have wonderful memories of our times together.

What my parents do not realize is that my sexual identity has been a life-long process. I remember being attracted to boys when I was in elementary school. I liked them differently than the girls. The girls were my closest friends. I always knew something was different,

Though we were both little boys, as my brother and I grew older, our differences began to emerge. We played sports together for a while—soccer and lacrosse, but it did not take long for me to see that sports were not for me and I began to develop other interests. My brother was a lot more like my dad, focused on most sports, surfing, and technology. I would go to my dad with a question about history or if I needed to assemble something, or computer technology. I was more like my mom. We shared a love for reading, playing tennis, and baking. I was also a computer nerd.

When I started middle school, my interests expanded to include the arts. I joined the poetry club, which was quite an eclectic group—many theatre-types. This was the first time I had ever had friends outside of sports. The poetry club exposed me to a whole new group of people and I found that I really enjoyed it. I developed some close friendships. It was around this time that my musical ability emerged and I started playing the piano and flute.

It was also in middle school that my sexual identity became stronger. I tried to suppress what I was experiencing. I would plan to deal with it later.

Our family moved prior to going to high school. I was not at all looking forward to attending a private all-male school. Girls had been my best friends to this point. I connected with them. The school was just as I anticipated—hyper-masculine, heteronormative culture that focused on being exceptional at sports. So, I spent much of my time reading, playing tennis, and baking. I baked outside of school whenever I was stressed. I would bake late at night and watch sci-fi movies until as late as three in the morning. I also joined a Robotics Club because it gave me a chance to hang out with a fun group of guys. While they were interested in athletics, it was not their entire life. Learning bits of coding and how to put together robotic components was fun, too.

I tried to date a girl when I was in tenth grade. It was very short-lived. She had been a close friend. We saw one movie, texted a few times and that was the end of it. She really did not feel much like a girlfriend.

We were church-goers but what I remember most about it is the negativity toward same-sex attraction. The message I received was that homosexuality was not a good thing. It made me feel very uncomfortable and affected the way I saw myself. So, I stopped going.

After I told my parents about my being gay, I needed to tell my extended family. The conversation with my paternal grandmother went well. She was surprised but she was kind and loving. My mom told the remainder of her family but their exposure to the LGBTQ community is very limited…me, but they have been fine. It is hurtful to think that my dad has still not shared about my being gay with anyone in his family.

I went to a very small college of two thousand students. That limited my exposure to other gay people, so I did not date at all. The pool of people I would like to have dated was small. However, in terms of LGBTQ people, you could never be sure who was straight, bi, or gay. There were a fair amount of queer people for the number of students there. Everyone was very accepting. I majored in international relations and economics so that kept me busy enough for four years.

I met my partner, Andrew, on a dating site the summer before my junior year of college. He was in seminary at the time. Andrew has been a wonderful source of encouragement to me. I can tell him anything and not feel judged. He is the one person in my life who I feel is truly family. We have been together for three years, now.

There have been times over the last few years when I've felt more comfortable around Andrew's family rather than my own because I know where they stand with my sexuality. They are religious too but in a different way from my family.

My grandmother has really tried and always makes a point to ask about Andrew. "How is your friend?" The friend comments are a sort of sad victory because while she asks about him, she relegates his status as my significant other and partner to a "friend." This detracts from who he really is to me. It could be a generational thing, or it could be due to my family having relatively zero exposure to LGBTQ people besides myself, or from passive homophobia.

As far as discrimination is concerned, I have received less than most people, since that dreaded day in Ecuador. When I interviewed for jobs, I was afraid that I would experience discrimination but I did not. It was a relief to see diversity and equality in the workplace.

I have become comfortable with my identity but there is reconciliation that needs to take place in my relationship with my parents. There are many things that I need to say to them. It is hurtful to me that they have never asked to hear my story. This has been a significant part of my life—that they are unaware. Their reaction to my coming out was wounding and I struggle with anger toward them. But, I come from a family where conflict is avoided and often conversations never happen. I may need to be the one to begin this one.

I find that my parents have each responded to my life differently. My dad and I seem to argue more now...mostly about politics. He loves to argue about politics. I wonder if it is a response to my lifestyle. My mom has been really trying to make an effort. She seems much more at ease and sincerely tries to befriend Andrew. My dad appears uncomfortable around him. I know he would really like to get to know my family better. I just do not know when that will happen.

Since Andrew is in seminary, I find myself attending church now and then when he is speaking and asks me to come. The awkwardness that I felt from church in the past comes to mind and I try to resist having those same thoughts of not feeling accepted. I have gone to a few talks at the seminary. One really stood out to me. It was about Biblical history and homosexuality and talked about how all the gospels fit together and what they are trying to say. It was encouraging. It crushed some of the narratives that have been built up in fundamental religions. I've read books which have also had a big influence on my thinking and have been very healing to me.

I have learned that who I am really matters. My happiness is important and living my true self is all part of that being realized.

*Eric lives in the mid-west and works as an assistant bank examiner. His partner, Andrew, lives nearby and has completed his seminary degree and is awaiting an assignment by the church.*

# Boomie

## Chapter 8

*Boomie has always been a homebody, placing God, family, and loyal friends first. Home and the familiar provided comfort for her. So, when her best friend's mother, died in a gruesome car accident when she was in kindergarten, Boomie was greatly affected. She was already an anxious child and this incident was traumatic for her. The woman was her mother's best friend, so they mourned the loss together.*

*After the funeral and the shock of the accident had lessened, Boomie was frightened all the time. She would be fine at home but as soon as the word "school" was mentioned, she would become physically sick. She would shake, sweat, and become disoriented. Her stomach would hurt from being so anxious that she would vomit, and she was terrified of vomiting. It became an entire body experience, like a panic attack. Those occurred much later in life.*

### Boomie's Story

I am confident that the genesis of my nervousness was due to this tragic car accident. It really shook my five-year-old brain. I remember being constantly afraid that my mom would also die in a car accident while I was at school, like my friend's mom did. So, I believed that if

I could find ways to be with my mom all the time then that might not happen. So, my way of dealing with the fear was that I was constantly trying to find ways to leave school to be with at least one of my parents. I even tried running away from school several times and the janitor would catch me. I had my "getaway" all mapped out in my mind. So, vomiting and running became a vicious cycle for me! Eventually, the anxiety and impulsivity became debilitating, and it was time to seek professional help. Three years later, I was diagnosed with *severe* obsessive-compulsive disorder and generalized anxiety at the age of eight.

My mind was always very busy. I spent a great deal of time thinking about my situation, attempting to problem solve it away. I was self-aware and even at a young age I attempted to figure out who I was. I remember feeling different from the other girls and noticed an unusual attraction to them when I was in third grade. I thought I felt that way because I admired them. They *were* super cool. I liked them, but differently. I had crushes on them and was obsessive about being friends with them. I would do things for them that typically only couples do for each other—calling and texting every day and writing sweet long notes. I always tried to be in their sight of vision at school and hid behind my attraction through friendships. I had a difficult time making friends and most of my friendships did not end well! Looking back, I believe that I was unsuccessful in this area because I was frustrated. This frustration contributed to my anxiety and overpowering OCD. Had I known how to identify what I was feeling, I just might have been able to avoid some of the pain that I experienced.

Although my family was supportive, I did not know how to describe what was going on inside of me. So, I internalized everything and became adept at concealing my anxiety. That was only a temporary solution. It all came out as I got older.

Because I was teased, whispered about, and bullied by the girls, I started hanging out with the boys. It was a quick fix and not too noticeable. I loved sports, as they did, and I could relate to them through that. In fact, I was a lot better at sports than most of the boys my age and would typically be picked first for teams. I was accepted and found comfort in my sports friendships with the boys.

In fourth grade, I continued to be terrified of school, so my parents developed an incentive program to encourage me to go. It worked! I was rewarded a dollar for each day I went to school. I refused to be overcome by my fear, so later that school year, I earned enough to buy a Nintendo 64. That Nintendo 64 is a huge symbol of success and perseverance. I will never give it away because of what it represents. To this day, it's in my home.

I also had to learn that when I was afraid and my parents couldn't come to my immediate aid, I could lean on God. This realization was monumental in my faith. I had to learn to be independently strong and understand that my parents were only human, and I had to have another form of support to lean on when I was feeling alone and anxious.

I was born into a very privileged, intelligent family with five children. I was the fourth girl. My oldest sister is a lawyer for the United Nations and is now getting leadership and managerial experience in the non-profit medical field overseas. The second oldest sister is an ordained minister. My third sister is a clinical child psychologist. My younger brother is currently in medical school. We were always very close.

My parents are wonderful people. They share all responsibilities equally. Both mom and dad took out the trash, did the shopping, cooked, changed diapers and cleaned. Mom stayed home to raise us and went back to teaching later. She is still teaching today! My dad is a pediatrician and business owner and has been in private practice for over thirty years.

My parents came from very different social classes but were always unified in their ideas about how to raise their children. My mom grew up poor and was one of five children. Dad was privileged but always a very hard worker. My siblings and I knew that even though our family had more than enough we should have no expectations when it came to material things. We had to earn what was given to us. Our parents did not want their children to grow up to be "brats." They had many rules for us because they wanted us to learn to be responsible. We learned the value of hard work by being required to get jobs during the summer when we reached age fourteen. I taught swimming lessons for eight years. I learned to save money and to take responsibility for some of my own expenses. I helped pay for some of my college and my car, among other things. Nothing other than birthday or Christmas gifts were just handed to us.

In addition to our summer jobs, we were also required to read every day, to tithe to our church, and to do chores. I felt a lot of pressure at times, but my parents always had our best interest at heart and, overall, have done an outstanding job with their kids. They encouraged us to be ourselves. We learned to be accountable in every sense and sometimes had to learn it the hard way when we refused to listen to sound advice or were impulsive!

We also had to earn my parents' trust. As we got older, we were given more freedom and had to learn to be responsible and continue to meet their expectations. While we were given the chance to choose freely, we never doubted what was expected of us. Even when we messed up, we would come through hard situations with more wisdom and confidence because of my parents' guidance. They allowed us the opportunities to make decisions. From this we learned to choose wisely.

Our family has always been humor driven. Life is rough sometimes. Laughing is therapeutic in my family so we tried to find whatever good there was in any given situation. Everyone is witty and sarcastic in their own way. So, even when we question whether someone is joking or being real, it doesn't matter... we deal! Both of my parents are hilariously quirky so none of us had a chance of being otherwise. We learned that the tough times will inevitably come regardless of how hard we try to avoid them and that laughing and "faking it until you're making it" was the best in the long run.

We traveled a great deal as a family in the Summer. I believe our family is close today because of that time together. Although this was a privileged perk and we visited awesome places, my parents made sure that they balanced the relaxation with learning. We would visit national parks and before each one we would go to the visitor's center to read about the history of what we were going to see. No kidding! We would often be quizzed! We even had the nerdy workbooks to do during long car rides.

I loved all outdoor activities and would stay outside for hours at a time. I thrived on playing alone. My mind could wander and I could do whatever I wanted with no agenda or input. One of my favorite memories was trying to build a teepee. Most of the time, I would play in my yard at home and occasionally would play with neighbors who were of similar age. I still preferred to play with boys rather than girls because dolls were pointless and Legos were just awesome. I knew this preference set me apart but I didn't mind. I was doing what I loved. I learned to really appreciate discovering new things on my own and that gave me confidence.

Some of my happiest moments as a child revolved around playing sports. I was an athlete and won many awards for my skill. I have always been a big collector of "things" and my trophies were one of those collections I admired. I knew while I was dealing with all my mind turmoil that I was a female anomaly and that most girls didn't enjoy sports like I did. I was a competitor. In fact, people probably knew I was a lesbian before I did. I joke, but truly, I think that was a possibility! Sports and being outdoors were a safe-haven for me. I could get away from worrying. Unfortunately, I did not like being "coached." I wanted to do my own thing, so that brought along some interesting dynamics at times. Regardless, sports were always my favorite pastime whether I was playing or being a spectator, outdoor or indoor. I felt confident and assured as a player so I clung to this hobby. Even my clothes were sporty. I wore everything from Nike to Adidas, top to bottom.

My collecting was a hobby that included a broad range of things: all kinds of gadgets and watches, pens and pencils, sports cards and collector series cards (Pokémon), POGS, Micro Machines, Legos, Playmobiles, Hot Wheels, etc. I liked to take things apart and put them back together. I would find whatever random supplies I could at home and put them all together to make a masterpiece. I ended up breaking many things this way...which was not so good!! I never used directions because I thought they were "stupid" and I didn't like anyone telling me how to play. I was a rogue. I never liked following rules. I just didn't care. I have always walked a line between semi-apathy and confidence. I don't really know how to explain it. But, I could busy my mind with these activities and I taught myself many different trades, trouble-shooting with electronics, putting different toys together to make one big toy, taking apart watches and figuring out how all the pieces worked together. I became a go-to person. This knowledge gave me a sense of self-assurance and motivation.

I was a huge tomboy and unashamedly so. I would describe myself as a "pretty tomboy." I am clean cut, big on hygiene, and I smartly put outfits together...not at all "butch." I have never been a girly-girl and still despise "dressing up." Why would I want to be uncomfortable on purpose? Interestingly, I was not attracted to girls like me. I was attracted to "girly" sporty girls. Does that make any sense at all? I have felt that way from a very young age.

I grew up going to a Baptist church every Sunday. We didn't have an option as to whether we would go to church or not. When our church split from the Southern Baptist Convention to become the Cooperative Baptist Fellowship, we followed. Our former church wouldn't allow women deacons or female ordained ministers to preach. After joining another church, both of my parents became deacons and have preached from the pulpit. My ideas of church were always inclusive of all people. My entire family are feminists, especially my dad and my younger brother. It was a pretty good church fit.

I loved vacation Bible school every summer. I looked forward to it and would go voluntarily. It wasn't "school" so that was a plus. I was interested in learning about the Bible and I loved all the songs we would sing and the crafts. Creativity and learning were healthy outlets for me and helped me to get my mind off other things. My mom was the teacher for the fifth to eighth grade group. She was tough, but we learned a lot. I really enjoyed helping with the children's church that met after Sunday school when I got older. I would assist the teachers with the kids and help with the babies in the nursery. I developed a love for being in community with kids and they looked up to me. To this day people say I have a unique way with kids. They like me, it's a lot of fun to be with them, and very humbling. Kids get it and their perceptiveness is second to none.

When it comes to what "religion" I am, I do not claim a denomination. I consider myself a Christian first, not a Baptist. Who cares what denomination you are? That's not what's important.

I was baptized when I was in fifth grade. I chose this. I felt assured and was confident in my personal relationship with Jesus. Especially after the realization I had in fourth grade that I absolutely needed a personal relationship with Jesus. I knew this was the direction I wanted to go. I spoke to the current pastor about what baptism meant and how it related to my faith journey. I felt no resistance to get baptized. Because I couldn't inwardly understand my thoughts and feelings related to attraction, I certainly was unable to talk to God about them. I thought that being baptized may be a good way to open-up communication about that, publicly committing myself to Him. Obviously, I saw myself as different. So, I chose to follow through with being baptized and wanted my church family to support me in that decision. They did.

Shortly after my baptism, I began to experience more obvious same sex attraction in my relationships at school. Fortunately, I didn't negatively relate my attraction to girls with my baptism. I don't know that I could have handled the anxiety that would have come with that. It was too complex.

Middle school was even more difficult than elementary school. At least in elementary school, I would be able to make it through the day without having to go home, but this just meant I'd spend the rest of the day weeping about how mean everyone was to me. In middle school, I was overweight due to several mental health medicines I was taking, so this made me an easier target for being teased. Middle school brought a whole new set of problems.

When I was in seventh grade, I was homeschooled the last few months of the school year because of a cyberbullying incident that caused debilitating anxiety in me. Middle school kids are just mean. It is a miserable time for just about everyone but for someone like me, it was unbearable. One afternoon during music class, I overheard some boys laughing hysterically and high-fiving about having told a mentally challenged boy to go home and shave his eyebrows... and he did. They even had the boy laughing with them! That was wrong and I wanted to stick up for this boy, so when I heard about it, I reported what they had done. Their actions made me sick to my already anxious stomach. It was the least I could do. This sweet, innocent boy was a friend of mine and I wanted to protect his dignity. The boys eventually heard that I had reported them and quickly made and distributed a hate website about my two girlfriends and me. It said, "Sign here if you hate _____, _____, & _____." A virtual hit list? And this was before cyberbullying was even a thing! Our yearbook pictures were shown with devil horns drawn on our heads. Almost our entire class had signed it. I was mortified, I had absolutely done the right thing and I deserved this? I didn't know what to do with the public embarrassment that I had experienced from the website. My parents were not happy and went into protection mode. They immediately went to the boy's parents to say that they were going to give the boy a chance to take down the website or they would be talking to the police. They started legal action by filing a police report and made sure each parent knew that the next knock on their door wasn't going to be an angry parent. It would be the police. The website was taken down, but that was only an outward action. Inwardly, that experience ruined me for two years. People who I thought were my friends turned against me. I could not finish seventh grade. I only went back for my end of the year academic awards ceremony because I had received an award for my writing. My mom went with me because I was terrified. I had no idea what the boys would do to me. I became even more frightened to go to school. The administration of the school did nothing about this incident.

In middle school, like most teens, I acted like I had boyfriends. I'd write them notes with rules they should follow; i.e. no cussing, must go to church. I would write the boys love letters because I thought that was the normal thing to do but didn't "date" them. I did not date until high school.

In high school, I had two boyfriends, but the relationships felt awkward and forced. Interestingly but not surprisingly, I tried to stay friends with my old boyfriends. I felt more comfortable being myself with boys, so it seemed normal to me. I mean my first kiss wasn't until I was sixteen while at summer church camp so clearly, I was fine just being friends.

Tragically, when I was in high school, my youth pastor committed suicide. My dad's family owned a lot of farmland. The youth pastor went to the home on the farmland and hung himself from the deck, for all his neighbors to see. Later, we discovered that he had struggled with depression in the past. He seemed like he was doing well. He was married and very young. I was a student leader at the time and on the youth committee that hired him. It was difficult to help support the students through this when I did not understand it myself. Unfortunately, I was the only senior and so by default, the oldest person in my youth group, so I took it hard feeling like I had to fix what had happened. It was speculated that his depression had returned and he told no one about it. Even for those who knew him best, this was unexpected. It was quite a shock to the church.

In high school, I devoted much of my time to my sports—tennis and swimming. I went to state for both sports. I intentionally stayed pretty busy. I declined a minor tennis scholarship to college because I chose to focus on my studies and have time to socialize.

In college, I majored in communication and media studies and minored in psychology, graduating in four years. I worked very hard to have friends. I was getting more attention from boys than I ever had and for the first time I was flattered, but not because I was attracted to them. It was just nice to divert my attention from how I was really feeling and what I was beginning to believe about my sexuality. I attempted to suppress what I believed might be my actual identity by kissing a lot of boys. I did not mean anything by it but it created a whole host of rumors about me, as a result. Crude nicknames were said and friends talked behind my back. I decided to try not to beat myself up about it. So, when I dated, it never went anywhere. We were just like best friends. I was attracted to the guys because they were good people. So, after we broke up, we remained friends. I have never had an issue saying men are good-looking, but I don't want to have sex with them. This is where attraction part comes in. It was around this time that I became increasingly more attracted to girls.

Along with studying and socializing, I spent much of my time playing intramural sports. I was even head referee and head intramural supervisor for the campus. This was one of my favorite jobs and very good experience.

During my college summer break, before my senior year, I worked as a Bible study leader for a church camp. There was one very specific incident that happened two to three weeks before heading to camp that affected me for the entire summer. I had gone to see a guy friend of mine. We were "attracted" to each other and drank much too much that night. I liked his attention but remember telling him, after we'd been kissing for a while, that I didn't want to have sex with him. He told me it would be good and that I should let him anyway. I can't remember much after that but I don't think he listened to me. I didn't stand up for myself like I should have.

The first week of church camp training, I freaked out and thought that I was pregnant with his child. I beat myself up thinking, "Why would I be qualified to teach kids about the Bible if I couldn't even behave myself? I'm a terrible influence! I am so unworthy." I had my first and second panic attack during training and had to talk to my parents every day, several times a day. They made sure that I understood the poor decisions I had made but assured me that all would be well. If he had raped me, my parents and I would have a lot to think about. They encouraged me not to let this incident affect my camp experience as best I could. To be certain, they had a package sent overnight to me with pregnancy tests! Of course, my mind had gotten the best of me, but I felt better knowing for sure that there was no baby. I was in correspondence with the guy about all of this and even he wasn't sure what happened that night. That didn't help. It was a frightening experience and I knew I never wanted to go through something like that again.

After that summer's scare, I tried harder to remember to take care of myself first, especially when drinking. I was ashamed to be having these feelings and even more ashamed of what people might think of me. I see now that I was lying to myself about wanting a family with a boy. I liked him as a friend but I didn't want to be with him. We just made some bad decisions. This experience helped me see while I was still in college that being with boys just didn't feel right on so many different levels! It ended up being one of the most memorable summers of my life. I grew so much in my faith and learned to lean on God when I didn't have anyone else.

After college, at age twenty-two, I found myself in a very abusive relationship. He was going to seminary at the same time as I was. We began dating my senior year right before I moved to where I'd be going to seminary. Shortly after the move, he became abusive toward me in every way—emotionally and physically, to the point of rape, and more than once. I put up with it for a while because I thought maybe I deserved this or wondered if this was normal. When I couldn't stand it any longer, I left everything. I left my full scholarship to seminary, my pool manager-head lifeguard job, my friends (albeit terrible people), my apartment, the city I'd fallen in love with, my church community, and my new puppy. I now realize that I escaped the most unhealthy time of my life. He made me feel ashamed about taking mental health medication, and for wanting to have safe sex, or for saying "no" when I didn't WANT sex. He also made me feel bad if I was tired and just needed to take a nap…after twelve-hour days at the pool and being dazed from heat exhaustion. This depressed me. I was forced to take birth control in secret because he didn't want to wear protection. He called me a messy drunk when I couldn't "please" him. I would drink so much that I would blackout. Why wouldn't I? He was terrible. Fortunately, I finally had closure on this horrible experience last year, six years later. It was about time.

It was a terribly dark period of my life after leaving him. I felt like I failed. After such a messy breakup, I had to compartmentalize my feelings, separating my depressed feelings of relationship loss from the feelings that something else was off in my life. It took me several years, but eventually I realized I was not crying over him at all, or over the abuse or the leaving. I was crying because for the first time, I admitted to myself that I was not just sad. I was lost and searching.

I suppressed what ruminations I could but was very hard on myself. I would lament about being a fake person because of my "secret." I was *absolutely* hiding from myself for four years. More than I did in college, I was finally admitting that I was a lesbian and that was why I was struggling! My "plan" was to admit it to myself first, then God, then my parents and siblings. And, although I don't believe as so many Christians do that "everything happens for a reason" and that "God is testing me" or that "I'm learning something from hard times," those thoughts certainly crossed my mind as I tried to sort through the suffering and the "why, why, why?" I realized that I needed to put these awful experiences aside. I had to go forward and tried to think about and appreciate all the good things in my life, no matter how small, whenever the horrible thoughts would come to mind.

I was encouraged by my parents to come home to heal. They took me in, and after about six months of recovery time and a job overseas as a nanny to my eldest niece for three months, my dad hired me as the assistant office manager in his pediatric practice. I thought that this was temporary and wouldn't let myself appreciate it, but it has become a vocation that I am really enjoying. It is a calling. I am a leader. What seemingly once was an accidental placement due to unfortunate circumstances, has become one of the biggest God-sent gifts. I have grown into my role as a secretary and main phone operator. I deal with many psychiatric emergency triage calls and most of the complex conversations. I am doing "church" work and I am ministering to others. I'm not in seminary and I'm not in a church. WE are the church.

I have no regrets about leaving seminary. I excelled while there and learned a tremendous amount. It boosted my confidence and was instrumental in proving to myself that I could be successful. I have moved on to a new life and am just shy of completing an MBA in health care administration.

I had dated a few other guys after college. Things didn't feel right while dating them. I would have fun but I was not happy. Many of them I have remained friends with, and just enjoy their company.

Before I came out, I dabbled in online same-sex dating and spoke to a few women but only went on dates with two of them. I was so desperate to find companionship that I made lots of unwise decisions. I let myself be taken advantage of and "cat-fished" as it's called, by fake people on the site.

In October 2014, I decided to come out to my family. I came out to my brother and older sister (the psychologist, PhD) first. My brother, who is four years younger, had come out five years prior while he was in college. This gave me the confidence to come out, too. I obviously took my time. My brother and sister were very good listeners and offered wise counsel. They didn't treat me any differently after knowing about me, as most LGBTQ+ people fear might happen. This helped me realize that in being honest about my sexuality, I am being more of my authentic self and will be happier as a result. They made sure I felt safe and affirmed their love for me, and then assured me that their relationship with me had not changed. They were proud of my honesty and bravery and expressed genuine happiness for me. They advised that I really did not need to carry this alone and that I should be with someone that night. They asked that I go to see mom and dad and check in with them when I arrived at their house. I spent that night with my parents.

I spoke to my mom first about what I had discovered about myself while sitting in my childhood room. She cried and asked, "Are you sure? Are you ready to deal with this? You don't choose this kind of life, I know." Then she proceeded to tell me that she and my dad would fully support me.

On hearing the news, my dad got teary-eyed and told me that he just wanted me to be happy and safe. He said, "Our tears are not because we are sad or upset that you are gay. Our tears are because we know of the road to come and it's going to be hard and it's going to be long." They knew that there would be challenges ahead— fighting off prejudice, assumptions, bigotry, and "turn or burn" damning trajectories. My mom added that they were not disappointed in me nor were they afraid to share about me with their church, co-workers, and friends. They loved me and wanted me to be happy.

I had twenty-four years of ruminating to prepare me for this night. I was relieved that I did not receive the response that I anticipated. I was a little fearful that my dad would be less accepting of me because of his more conservative background, his status, and family connections in the community, but deep down I knew that fear wasn't realistic. He has always been a compassionate and sensitive man and is adored by all who know him, but still, as his child I wanted his support. I had also grown up hearing my dad make comments that were offensive like, "That looks gay" or "That looks so faggy." He didn't realize how hurtful those comments were. I didn't know how hurtful they were. Obviously, I feel differently now. But my parents have always been my biggest fans. I have been blessed. They seemed to know exactly what I needed to hear that night. They have always been extremely loving, perceptive, and very wise people.

So, to my surprise, I did not feel like a different person. I felt like a freer Boomie. It was so refreshing to experience such a freedom while knowing that I had always been this way. I had not been leading people on, I had been leading myself on, not giving myself a chance to live into all that I was. I finally set myself free and it was awesome.

After I came out, my parents studied the Bible even more and added biology to their study in order to understand more fully what it means to be gay. They now believe that being gay is something that is not chosen and that I am still beautifully and wonderfully made in God's image. They celebrate all that I am and will become. I believe this, too. No one would choose this, and yet so many learn to live into who they were born to be and embrace it. Some research even goes as far as to suggest that being LGBTQ is something you're genetically predisposed to. It's also been speculated that families with one LGBTQ child are more likely to have another LGBTQ sibling. This might be the case with my brother and me!

I informed my other siblings later about me but took my time; one and a half to two years, when I let my friends and "the public" know, aka Facebook.

One of the major reasons I came out when I did was because of an incident that occurred several years after college. Since I had moved home and was back in my hometown where my college was located, I became really involved with my sorority again as an alum. I developed a crush on a girl from my sorority who was several years younger. We hung out together for a while. Almost daily, she would sleep over and come do her homework at my house instead of on campus. She would wear my clothes and buy me gifts. Often, I would be the first person she would want to call about things. She would tell me everything and always wanted me around. She would introduce me as her hilarious best friend to her college friends in the sorority. We were just friends, but I knew I wanted her to be more than just a friend…and even highly suspected that she might be a lesbian as well. This only made things more difficult. I wasn't out but was strongly attracted to her and would daydream about her. I could not get her off my mind. I knew that letting her know how I felt was not an option. If I was not comfortable coming out during college and at the same college just a few years prior, then she would not be either, if my intuition was correct.

One night, she had to cancel our plans and I got really hurt. She gave a lame excuse and was acting strange. I knew something was wrong and got angry. She told me that people had been talking about me being gay and they thought we were dating because of all the time we spent together. I was really upset because I had not even admitted to myself that I was gay and now people were talking about me? I felt like my story had been told to me. I was called out and had not even had a say. I told my friend that I did not understand and that those things were hurtful and untrue. So that night, knowing how very true those rumors were, very angry and very drunk, I took a carpet cutter and cut myself deep on the wrist right through the tattoo that said, "Love Wins." This was symbolic, I guess? "Love Wins" has always been my favorite phrase but before I came out, I hadn't considered the possibility that this phrase could be a LGBTQ-themed mantra. Now this has become my fight song, my rallying cry. At the time, I felt cheated that someone else told the story that I was supposed to tell.

I called my parents for help. My father stitched me up, giving me thirteen stitches. My mom took me out to buy some long-sleeve shirts so my injury wouldn't be so obvious at work. I was sure to clarify later, for my own sake that I was not trying to kill myself. I certainly could have lost too much blood and died, being that I was so intoxicated. What's worse, is my OCD and impulsivity are so much worse when my guard is down and I don't have a "stop" in my brain to say, "Hey, maybe that's not a good idea."

I felt a little depressed after that incident. It really scared me, but I was relieved at the same time. This was the single most influential moment that led to my coming out. It was a breaking point and moving forward was not optional. Yes, I severely dislike the "everything happens for a reason" cop-out, but I do believe that whatever we do go through, God is in that with us and that even the most broken and tragic situations have redemptive potential. We can learn from trials and pick ourselves back up. It's not preferable but it's fair. I did not drink for two years after that incident. Since my impulse control is diminished from alcohol, I am very careful to drink responsibly and with others when I do. This was life-changing lesson for me.

My family has been great about my being gay. They are loving and want me to be happy and safe. They've always encouraged me to be myself regardless, unashamed. That is a gift. My parents have always been our greatest support… especially through life's biggest challenges. I think we would all attest to the fact that these times have made us stronger together and we are blessed to have gotten through the mess in a better light.

It would be easy to allow the church culture to make me feel unworthy of God's love. It could even make my family, who are rock stars, feel unworthy. But, I know that I will never be separated from the love of God. This assurance is simple yet profound. For the longest time, after my abusive relationship with my boyfriend, I despised all church anything. I was almost engaged to this abusive youth minister in seminary. And he is a man of God? Not to be judgmental, but I believe that a calling to be a disciple of Christ meant something more. Those individuals were held to a higher standard. This was not the case with him so I wanted nothing to do with a church service, congregation, etc. I was a Christian and I believed in God but I hated the institution of church.

My mom had a good response to my apathy and doubt, "The same people who sit in the pews are the same people who sit on bleachers at games. It's just that the expectations we have, and should have, of the people of God are higher, and that's why it hurts more when you're let down and disappointed. I would say that's why I've also felt the sting of hurt more from people I know through the church. Even so, church is still the place that best points me towards the ancient and holy light, and the narrow path of righteousness. It's because of said church and the teachings of Christ that I can recognize the wrong and sting of brash and insensitive comments and people." My mom's brilliant. I just need to remember that ministering and worshiping are not confined to church walls. I feel as if I'd always known this but speaking it out loud revived its truth and significance to me.

As far as coming out is concerned, everyone has their own timing. Even if someone takes that freedom from you, don't forfeit all your "power" and self-confidence by rushing into a defining label before you're ready. You're a part of the LGBTQ community but that doesn't define you. You're a person first and you just happen to be that way, baby! Don't carry that burden alone. Tell someone. Allow others to support you. Don't stop "believing."

I have learned to deal with discrimination by ignoring the hurtful and focusing on the things that are true about me. You know yourself the best. Don't let anyone else try to rewrite your story or diminish you with their words. Trust in the loyal friends that have encouraged you to be your authentic self. Live in community with those that love you.

If I would have known how my family would respond I probably would have come out sooner. Knowing that your family will be supportive, regardless, is so formative for an evolving psyche. When my brother came out, I was inspired to do so myself.

Interestingly, what I thought was a big secret was not, to many people. Although I have always known I was different and then later admitted I was a lesbian to myself, it was affirming to me that I was not alone in knowing I was gay. It was as if they were journeying with me. That was really comforting and still is. One specific person I'm close with, my therapist, told me that he has always known that I was a lesbian. This was when my fiancée came with me to a follow-up appointment a few weeks ago and I was bragging we were engaged. It was really sweet of him and it made us feel like we have always been doing the right thing and have promise of a joyous future together. He told me to live into it even more and to be happy. He was sure to tell me, too, that he had never seen me so happy and relaxed! This was truly a gift indeed.

I have learned that it is important to be the best version of yourself. You do not owe anyone anything. Do what you love and own it. You are loved because of the unique person that you are. God can bring healing for the hurt that we experience in our lives. You are worthy. Let yourself be loved by someone else. It's a real thing and you deserve it. Do what makes you come alive. Preserve your memories. Write your thoughts down when you're frustrated…it's a great way to help diffuse any complicated situation and you might even learn something. Enjoy the little things and take joys and sorrows in stride. Lots of clichés? I don't even like them, but hey, they wouldn't be clichés if some of them didn't hold some truth.

Lastly but most definitely not least, I'd love to mention my beautiful fiancée, "Reckless." For the first time in my life, I am in a loving relationship and feel content. It's really refreshing and it feels perfect. Each time we have taken a step to become more committed to one another, it just feels right. And the best thing is—it's healthy! We never expected such happiness to be possible. Both of us had been in terribly abusive relationships. We were pretty worn and apathetic when we started talking. This has become, without a doubt, the best experience of my life. I have been so blessed. Our faith walks have flourished as we have had to work through her coming out, dating, and getting engaged. We both say we don't deserve each other or to be so happy, but we remain thankful, and deep down we know how much we do deserve each other. We have grown so much as individuals and as a couple. Each of us have worked hard to be the people we are and it shows. We understand that we are eternally blessed and love being in community with others to empower them and encourage them to be their authentic selves. We live understanding that to be in a successful relationship, we take care of ourselves first, so we can take care of each other. We don't complete each other, we complement each other. Love wins.

*Boomie has become more of an activist for LGBTQ+ rights since the last presidential election's disappointment. She has helped plan the inaugural pride festival in her hometown and actively participates in its executive committee as social media chair. She lives with her fiancée, Reckless, in her hometown in the southeast. They plan to be married in summer 2018.*

# Brandon

## Chapter 9

*"Don't ask, don't tell!" That was the slogan promoted by his dad's employer. Brandon's dad was career Navy. So, when Brandon finally came out at age twenty, he was completely surprised by his dad's reaction. His dad was the one who never went to church. He considered himself a Christian but didn't fit the bill of what Brandon was told it looked like to be "born again;" church attendance, fellowship with Christians, and being a part of the life of the church. And yet, in that moment when Brandon really needed love, support, acceptance, grace, and mercy, his dad was the one who provided it.*

### Brandon's Story

I grew up in an independent, ultra-conservative, fundamentalist church. My mother was responsible for making sure my brother, who was five years younger, and I had a proper religious upbringing. My father rarely went to church. His family was not very religious, from what I understand. My paternal grandmother was a clairvoyant medium, which I think is a no-no in most conservative churches. Through the years, my mother and I "progressed" together from the ultra-conservative forms of fundamentalism to a slightly more liberal approach but still stayed on the conservative side of the fence.

Our family was very close. Because my father's career required that we move every three to four years, our family and faith were the few constant aspects of life. We depended on each other. Through the course of his career we lived in a few different states, spending much of the time in Virginia. He retired the same year I graduated from high school, 2000.

My mom was the most important person in my life. I was a momma's boy. We shared a deep friendship. She used to tell me that I was "born more mature" than she was when she had me. She was only nineteen when I was born. We talked about everything. She shared things with me that some would probably say a mother shouldn't share with a child. We had a tight bond throughout my entire life. Even during the rocky times when I was coming out, we remained close…and I loved that.

Dad and I were never very close, partly because his job took him out to sea for several months at a time. We were also very different. Dad had more in common with my brother and they understood each other. They were very close. But when I came out later in life, something happened to my relationship with my dad and we grew much closer.

My brother and I spent a great deal of time together growing up. I was the safe one and did not take many risks. I spent much of my time protecting him from injury. While I have never had a broken bone or so much as a cavity, he broke several bones and needed to be stitched up multiple times in his childhood. We did have fun despite all the injuries.

In elementary school, I always felt different from the other children. I was a loner and could feel isolated even when in a group. I was more of an observer than a participant and was often not actively involved with the other children. I spent most of my time with the adults because I found them much more interesting and I felt more comfortable with them. I have been called an "old soul" on many occasions.

I started to experience attraction to the same sex as early as five years old. I have a vivid memory of standing in line with the other kindergarteners about to go into our school and seeing a boy that I had a huge crush on. I remember looking at him and knowing I was feeling something for him. That's all I remember…me looking at him as we stood in line, feeling those feelings.

I have memories of playing pretend and dress-up, acting, singing, and dancing. One of my most vivid memories, where I felt the happiest and most like "me", was when I was playing with some neighborhood kids on the playground one day. I think I was between six and eight years old at the time. It was just a few of us. I don't even remember who they were or what they looked like. I just remember they were girls, and one of them had a small purse with a long strap. I put the purse over my shoulder and pretended to be Dorothy Zbornak from *The Golden Girls*. I have no idea how I even knew who that was, my grandma must have let me watch it with her. Mom sure wouldn't have let me watch that. I was tall, and mature, and proud—and an old woman. But at some point, I pushed all those interests aside. My love for music remained but instead of singing, I went into the band.

In middle school, I tried playing soccer but really did not like it, too much running, so I started playing the clarinet. I picked up the clarinet because my dad told me that his father used to play the clarinet. His father had died unexpectedly of heart failure before I was born. So, when I auditioned for band in sixth grade, the band teacher let me try out a clarinet. I was a natural. I had all the embouchure and breath support needed to play it. I remember clearly the band director turning the mouthpiece of the clarinet around so I could blow into it while he moved his fingers on the keys. I produced a beautiful sound. He was impressed, and that made me feel great about myself. For one, because I knew my dad would be proud. Two, because I did love music and finally found something I was good at and enjoyed. And three, my mom was excited to connect with the band director because when she met him they realized they had gone to high school together. It was a cool experience all around.

Other than band, seventh and eighth grades were not great. I was always picked on and had a difficult time understanding the other kids. They did not understand me either.

I remember when I was in eighth grade, the seniors from the area high school came to help with our band. I found myself strongly attracted to the drum major, who happened to be a guy. I tried to ignore those feelings and never told anyone about what I was experiencing.

When I got to high school, I finally hit my stride. I was in an environment with other peers who were older than me. Being in band allowed me the opportunity to be in classes with the seniors, so my freshman year, I became very popular with them. I even started semi-dating a girl. It didn't go very far, because she was also dating someone else…and some other not-so-obvious reasons at the time. But just as my popularity started to rise, the military moved us again. This time we moved to the area near my mom's family.

Church continued to be a major aspect of our lives. God was always part of my story from a young age. My mom says the earliest things I used to talk about involved becoming a preacher. That makes sense, not only from a calling standpoint, but in church the pastor was akin to a celebrity of sorts. You listen to him and never question. What kid wouldn't want that? I didn't seem to mind the fact that I was sheltered from almost everything—pop culture, secular music, TV, movies, etc.

I remember the feeling I had the moment I notably experienced the Holy Spirit. At that time, I called it my moment of salvation, or accepting Christ. I was about eight years old and had gone forward during an altar call at our church. I prayed the "sinner's prayer" with the prayer counselor, then got up to walk back to my seat. Walking back to my seat, I remember feeling filled with something much lighter. I smiled as I rounded the corner into the pew, as though I was outside my body looking at myself.

I professed a call to preach and work in ministry early on. I used to help teach Sunday school when I was in seventh and eighth grade. Then, I started an after-school Bible study at my public high school. When I was seventeen, my church needed a Sunday school teacher, so

I took over teaching first through third grade Sunday school for a year. Then, our choir director quit, so I took over leading the choir and the music program at the church. As a teenager, I was responsible for planning and rehearsing the choir each week, and for Easter and Christmas cantatas. Everything was done acapella; without instrumental musicians. Did I have great skill? No, but I had some natural talent and knew enough to help us sound pretty good in four-part harmony hymns. Accompaniment tracks were "of the devil," so our church thought, as was all modern music. Anything with drums was considered "Satan's instruments". Don't want to tempt people to dance…how evil!

I was so engrossed in my church that it made it easier to ignore what was going on in my body. I do remember hearing the hellfire and brimstone sermons about homosexuals from televangelists and my own pastors. Growing up, one of my pastors used to tell us the way we could identify a homosexual was by the earrings. "Left ear: not queer. Right ear: wrong ear. Both ears: woman."

As hard as I tried, however, I was unable to change my same-sex attraction. Near the end of high school, I started watching gay porn. We only had one computer in our house and I thought I had deleted my search history, but my mom and aunt used the computer and discovered the secret. When my mom confronted me on it, I denied it. This created a serious problem between my parents, because she thought my dad was the one watching gay porn. I can't even imagine what issues that must have created for them.

I started working at a theme park when I was sixteen and continued for several years. It was my favorite job ever. I worked my way up and got promoted quickly, three times over the course of two years. There were a lot of gay folks who worked as performers there, and in other areas of the park. Even while still attending my fundamentalist church and "being straight," I developed a crush on my supervisor who was gay. He was older than me by about five years and again, while I was still "straight," was my first gay kiss. It never grew into anything more, but it naturally created a lot more internal conflict for me.

I became good friends with many of my co-workers. I was closest to Sharon. She was a Christian and very open-minded, and we spent a great deal of time together. After going to the gym one day, we stopped at a Christian bookstore. Sharon told me that she recognized one of the guys working there from a gay bar that she had gone to. I went back to the bookstore later to meet the guy again. We struck up a conversation and started seeing each other. We fell in love very quickly, and our relationship was tumultuous to say the least. We were both from very strict churches and carried a burden of guilt about our relationship that made it very difficult to stay together. We were stuck in a cycle of dating, repenting of our relationship, breaking up, and then getting back together. It was very difficult.

In November of 2000, after my experience at the theme park and during a "repent" cycle with the guy I fell in love with, I joined the Army National Guard. I got back together with the guy before deploying and he told me he would wait for me. Just before I left we went into another "repent" cycle and didn't see each other again for many years. I went to basic training— "boot camp" and military police school and was mobilized shortly after on 9/11. A year later we deployed to Kuwait and then Iraq in 2003-2004.

Prior to boot camp in 2001, I tried telling my parents about my struggle with same-sex attraction. They were driving me to the Military Entrance Processing Station (MEPS), where I would do all the preliminary paperwork and medical checks, and head to basic training directly from there. I was in the back seat of our minivan and I kept leaning forward to start to tell them but I just could not do it. I wanted them to know that it was something I had been struggling with but was working on and trusted God had healed me. I never got it out that day.

While deployed the first time in 2003, I was working in lay-ministry with the soldiers in my unit as I always had. I had a core group of other fundamentalist Christian friends there with similar worldviews. At one point, I became so overwhelmed by my secret, feeling guilt and shame, that I decided I needed to tell my family.

Fortunately, the phone in our barracks had a long enough cord for me to pull it up on a nearby top bunk. I called home and started to cry when my mom picked up the phone. I don't remember my exact words, but it was something to the effect of, "I just wanted to tell you that I've been struggling with homosexuality, and I'm trying to be straight." My mom's only response was, "Talk to your father," and she handed him the phone. Then, I told my dad what I had been carrying around for so long. I remember hearing and feeling his voice change. It was one of pure love and acceptance, and he said, "That's okay, son, God still loves you!" After a moment, he added, "Now... don't tell anybody else." From a man who spent more than two decades in the military, that advice made sense. That's all I remember from that call. I later found out that they were on their way to a family picnic. It was the Fourth of July. Probably not the best timing.

I heard some years later, that my mom basically shut down at that point and did not talk to anyone for a week. It is understandable, I suppose. My revelation had a lot of implications for me, her, and her relationship with my dad after all the lying I'd done to cover my tracks.

Back in the barracks in Kuwait, I hung up the phone and felt immediate relief. It was good to get it off my chest even though I knew things would be rocky at home with mom. And despite my dad's warning, I soon shared my "struggles" with a few close Christian friends in my unit. I wanted them to help keep me accountable and on the "straight and narrow." I ordered a correspondence course to help me become and stay straight. It was from a ministry run by a man who said God healed him of his homosexuality, and he was now happily married to his wife, with no remnants of his former "lifestyle."

My relationship with my mom was pretty damaged for a while. For better or worse, I was seven thousand miles away, and being that it was the early 2000s, we didn't have much access to the internet. We communicated mainly through snail mail, and she shared her concerns to me through pen and paper. She expressed that she didn't want me to go to hell, and shared Bible passages with me typically used against homosexuality, saying she was praying for me, encouraging me in my work with the ex-gay correspondence course program.

I remained in the Middle East for eight more months. My unit moved north from Kuwait to Baghdad. Most of my unit there did not really connect with our chaplain. Somehow, I was among a lot of other fundamentalists of different flavors... and our chaplain was a woman. We tried not to talk about the whole "woman pastor" thing, even though some of the guys took issue with it. I got along well with her, though, and she trusted me and allowed me to lead chapel services for our midnight shift guys. So, every week for eight months I preached a midnight service on Sunday and a Wednesday night service as well. It was energizing and empowering and incredible.

After returning to the United States in August 2004, I enrolled at Liberty University, the late Jerry Falwell's conservative Christian institution. I started going to a church that had a ministry with recovery groups for people dealing with different issues—divorce, porn addiction, alcohol abuse, and *same-sex attraction.* I went to the same sex-attraction group for many months and participated with the others in the group. We kept each other accountable to having thoughts that were pure and "straight," and openly discussed our struggles. While I disagree with the premise of the group now, this was a big catalyst for me in just being able to speak openly about that part of my life with a group of people who shared similar struggles and could be empathetically supportive.

The summer after my first full year at Liberty, I was home visiting my parents and the phrase "gay theology" popped into my head as I sat at their computer. I searched it online and found a plethora of Christian websites showing their gay-affirming understanding of Scripture. I was blown away. I had no idea this existed before. I mean, I'd heard of "gay churches" but of course they were "ridiculous and satanic." But, these churches were engaging with Scripture. That started my year and a half of devouring everything I could to try to sort it all out.

I went to Liberty for one more semester before deciding to discontinue my studies. School was expensive and I didn't want to take out any more loans. I moved back to my hometown and eventually got my own place with a roommate.

In the next few months, I started leading praise and worship music for Wednesday night Bible study groups at the big southern Baptist church I was attending. I did that for several months until one day I got a text from my friend Alicia, saying that pastor James didn't want us to have music that night before we split into our separate men's and women's Bible studies, which was our norm.

Instantly, I sensed that he knew about me. "What was the big deal?" I thought to myself. After all, I had not made any decision about my sexuality yet. At that point, I had just been reading and praying and researching and looking at Greek and Hebrew and trying to prayerfully, diligently sort things out. I wasn't dating. I wasn't having sex. I was just trying to understand things.

That night, I went to Bible study late, hoping to sneak in and avoid any conversations. But of course, pastor

James wasn't in Bible study; he was in his office waiting for me to walk by as I entered the church, so I walked into his office.

It was the typical, non-question question from PJ: "So, how's everything going?"

"Great," I said.

"Anything going on you want to talk about?" He asked.

"No, not really—I'm good. How are you?" I replied.

He was going to have to say whatever he wanted to say. I was not hiding anything, and I was not doing anything. I didn't have anything I wanted to talk with him about because I knew how he would respond and I'd already read everything on that side of the argument. He basically let me know that it had come to his attention that I seemed to have a lot of gay friends on *MySpace.*

I explained to him, openly, where I was, what I was feeling, and how I was prayerfully researching and reading and analyzing Scripture. I expressed that I had not come to any conclusions yet. I'll never forget his response.

"I think you know what the truth is here, and you're just fighting it. The problem with sitting on the fence for so long, is that one day you're going to fall down and you're going to hurt yourself."

Thanks for that, pastor James. Thanks for bringing my genitals into the conversation and for having them crushed. I don't remember what awkward conversation ended that dialogue, but I left the church, got into my car, and just drove around for a while. There was much mental back-and-forth, and many of tears that night.

Everything I'd been reading and all the beautiful LGBT Christians I'd been fellowshipping with in online chat rooms and prayer groups deeply resonated with me. In the physical world, I knew I loved this church community. They were my family. I felt at home there, and how could that be wrong?

I made the decision that night. I would walk away from all this searching, and just accept the fact that my church was right, and that "gay Christianity" was a delusion. I couldn't give up the church family and community I had. I was straight, and that was that.

Later that evening when I got home, I logged into the computer to the website for a gay Christian ministry. I had become so active in participating in their online discussion groups, email prayer chains, and had been writing daily devotions for their email list for some time now.

Their founder and still current leader, Mary, was such a beautiful model of Christ's love to me.

"No," I said to myself. "*This* is not wrong. These people all love God and live like Jesus more than some of the other 'Christians' I know. I am gay." And that was that. As quickly as I "decided" to go against my soul and be straight, I decided I was wrong and followed my heart and intuition.

I later found out that I immediately became a hot topic in the Bible study and prayer circles at the church. I was apparently a "big scandal." A couple of the guys from Bible study reached out to me, especially after I announced not too long thereafter that I was moving to Los Angeles. One wanted to have breakfast with me before I left. We did. He just wanted to say goodbye and make sure that I had seen a few of these Bible passages I may have missed. I moved to Los Angeles in July 2007 where I joined the army reserves.

After I came out as a self-affirming gay Christian, a few years passed and mom had come to terms with things. We still loved each other very much and spoke regularly throughout all of this. At that point, she still didn't agree with the "lifestyle" but was loving and kind. Dad never cared either way. The fact that he had three gay siblings probably helped some. I had met and spent time with my aunts and uncles, but we never spoke about their relationships. Even my aunt's long-time partner was included as part of the family, yet the relationship was never identified. It's incredible what we can avoid. Of course, when I came out, my aunt and her partner were just like, "Oh, thank God. We've been waiting for years."

About six years after I came out as being gay to my parents for the second time, not as just struggling with my sexuality, mom got to the point where she was open to meeting more people from my world and learning more about same sex attraction. I'd become heavily involved with the Gay Christian Network, which hosts a conference in a different spot around the U.S. every January. In January of 2013, she flew to meet me in Los Angeles, and we took a mother-son road trip to Phoenix, where the conference was held that year. That conference opened her eyes and heart in many ways. It does for pretty much everyone who steps into that conference center and takes part in the corporate worship led at the start of each conference.

Time and time again, you would find parents who were formerly non-affirming, or "sitting on the fence" about what to think, standing up along with the hundreds of other souls in that room, singing, praising God, praying, crying, submitting their lives to Christ and to leading lives of love. Mom was no different. She started connecting with more people there and became fast friends with a lot of my friends, leading to her texting them more than I even did after the conference.

When mom attended the next conference with me in Chicago in 2014, she opened up even more. She made it a point to pull me aside, tell me she loved me, and let me know that she affirmed me for who I was.

I moved to New York to complete a degree in American studies in January 2014. Mom developed a highly aggressive form of breast cancer while I was away, so I returned home often to spend time with her. I missed many classes and was given many extensions for finals and papers but mom and I had some beautiful moments together. She died in January 2016. I returned to my studies and completed my B.A. in May 2016. She would have been very proud.

Much has happened since then. My mom and I were very close, and her death was a significant emotional event for me. It caused me to question everything. I had never lost anyone so close. I became more open and began to question my own spirituality. What did I really believe, concerning life after death, and my own spirituality in general?

I often wonder what life would have been like if I had grown up in a more mainline, liberal denomination. My faith background made a huge difference in delaying my coming out. How far could I have gone, tapping into my truest self sooner in life? Where would I be now?

Throughout my military career, I had a desire to study and become a chaplain. I was involved in some sort of lay ministry wherever I went, and it made sense to me to stay in the military and have that be my career. But after I came out, I knew I needed to find an LGBT-affirming seminary. Last year, I finally finished the undergraduate degree I'd started so long ago and was accepted at Yale's Divinity School. I was preparing to attend to start earning my master's in divinity, the graduate degree required for military chaplains, when I realized that the career that I had recently started building as a life and leadership development coach was fulfilling more of my yearnings and callings than I thought it would. I was working with people to identify happier, more passionately creative ways of living, and along with my new position as an equal opportunity advisor in the Army Reserve. I was fulfilling my own desires to encourage others to live their God-given, truest selves in this world.

The military has given me so many opportunities to develop into the person I was created to be, in kind of roundabout ways. Strangely enough, I believe I would never have joined the military if I would have been out as a gay man. I think my reasons for joining were largely connected to my desire to find acceptance in a performance of masculinity that was not actually me. So, deploying again to Baghdad in 2009-2010 under "Don't ask, don't tell" after I was already "out" in the civilian world, was quite an experience. I had to cram myself back into the closet for deployment. It was difficult and very annoying. Thankfully I worked with a bunch of creative people in radio and television broadcasting at the time, so for the most part it was not an issue...except for my direct supervisor. He was kind of an oddball of a conservative Christian, who made left field comments in the office all the time. "If they ever let gays in the military, I'm getting out," he would say, sitting about three feet from me. I did not go to any great lengths to hide anything. It was an annoyance for me at best. I just "didn't tell" and they "didn't ask." It was like the big, awkward elephant in the room. My supervisor could push in that way knowing I could not really say anything. Thankfully, I was well-versed in Scripture, much more so than he was, so we had some interesting non-work-related discussions in the office. Most of the time, though, I just rolled my eyes and continued my work, while my coworkers just stared at me whenever he made a comment. They were all equally annoyed for me and wondered how I would respond.

I have learned that everyone has their own journey to walk. Coming out must be done according to your own timing. When you do come out, have a back-up plan. Make sure you are physically safe and stable. You could be potentially compromising your living, working, food, and shelter situation. Start by coming out to people or a community you know will be supportive. You will need that support. Even if you live in the "boonies," find online support. As much as possible, do not attach yourself to any outcome. You can only control your own thoughts and actions. You have no control over how others will respond. Their response is not about you; it's about *them*. You don't have to prove anything to anyone. You just need to be yourself. You are here for a purpose. The best way to find and live your purpose is to listen to yourself, to your biggest, truest, highest desires and callings. Respond openly and gratefully to them, wherever they might take you. You may feel guilty if you leave certain people or communities for your own mental health and livelihood. You may feel the need to somehow go back and save them from their ignorance and prove to them that you are still the same person, to prove your worthiness of their love, to show them that you are right, that you can be "gay and ____" (Christian, for example). In the quest to prove your point, you may be tempted to contort yourself to fit into some other boxes where you do not belong, in boxes that will become just as constrictive as the closet you just fought so hard to come out of. Be patient, be loving, be gentle with yourself.

When I look back on my situation, I wonder how I could have done things differently. Part of me wishes I had given my family a chance to walk with me on my eighteen-month journey of prayer, research, and discovery of my identity. I went from "God wants me to be straight" to "No, I am actually designed this way." But, I did not trust anyone or give anyone a chance. On the other hand, when I did finally come out, many of their responses were telling. If I had not been as far along in my research and heard them give such dismissive responses, it may have taken me even longer to come out. They would have been examining everything I did. It was hard enough to "hide" when people were not actively watching me. Ultimately, I believe that if I had known how supportive my loved ones could have been, I would have come out sooner.

My deepest desire is to live a life of love, openness, and non-judgment. My focus is on becoming all that I was created to be by exploring creativity and gender and helping others to do the same.

*Brandon is a life and leadership development coach in the southeast. He works with creative people who are in non-creative or otherwise unfulfilling careers, helping them to discover what they want to be to express their truest self and passions. Brandon is also an equal opportunity advisor in the Army Reserve. He works with leaders to provide education and training events to eradicate discrimination, celebrate and maximize diversity and inclusion, and resolve conflict.*

# Laura

## Chapter 10

*Laura was born in the 1950s, so while she was growing up, being gay was never a topic of discussion. If it was talked about it was done in a whisper. The societal and religious views on being gay at the time, her family's position within the social strata, and upholding the family name, allowed her no opportunities to share what she was feeling. She grew up believing that being gay was wrong. Even though she knew from an early age that she was going to marry a woman, Laura was too afraid to embrace who she really was. She did what was expected of her, remaining "hidden in a closet" until she was in her mid-thirties.*

### Laura's Story

I was a tomboy from the beginning. I hated wearing dresses because they made me feel awkward and uncomfortable, so I spent most of my time in pants and shorts. I was never allowed to wear jeans because my grandparents were upper class and high society did not permit it, so I was told. My interests were more in line with what boys would like. I loved to play sports, dressed in a cowboy outfit instead of a cowgirl, and I played with my favorite wood burning set. I did have my favorite dolls, but I never played with them like other girls did. I, also, liked to work in the garden with my grandfather.

I am grateful to my parents for giving me life. At a young age, they were trapped in a life defined by the societal and familial expectations to marry well. They did the best they could then divorced when I was four years old. I was their only child.

I saw little of my father after the divorce. He remarried, right away, the woman with whom he had an affair. My first half-brother was born a few months later. His new family was underway. My half-sister and another half-brother followed. There seemed no time for me. I could count on one hand the number of times I saw my father before my mother and I moved to Florida when I was nine.

So, I was raised by my mother, along with my maternal grandparents, to some extent.

We lived close to my grandparents, so I have many fond memories with them. I would spend delightful summers at their house while my mother worked. There were many kids my age in their neighborhood, so I developed some close friendships and had lots of playtime. My grandmother bought me a little pool for their backyard, which made the summer extra fun.

I was very close to my grandmother and she took great care of me. I loved being with her for the most part. She and I would play card games and build tall houses out of them. She would entertain me by taking me to wonderful places—the movies, downtown Baltimore on the small green school bus, and lunch at Hutzler's tea room. One time, she invited my third-grade teacher, a very kind and caring person, to join us. I think my grandmother appreciated her taking an interest in my well-being. I might have had a little crush on her, too!! I remember being sick for an entire month during the school year with the flu, then measles, then German measles and finally the mumps, thank heaven only on one side. My grandmother nursed me back to health and worked with me to keep up my schoolwork.

There were rough times with my grandmother, also. She would teach me manners and etiquette. I often learned this the hard way, especially when my mouth and behavior were not to her liking. Having good manners and respecting others was important to her so she passed that value along to me. She was a very loving and supportive woman who encouraged me to follow my heart, to do what was right for me.

My grandfather was very different from my grandmother. He was a professional man, judgmental, and pretty opinionated about what he thought was right. He was clear, what he said was the only right way to think and feel. We clashed often around that when I was older.

I did have some special moments with my grandfather. I loved the many hours we spent working on the yard and in the garden beds. He had quite a green thumb and creative ability and taught me many lessons about gardening.

My grandfather was a drinker and had quite a reputation for his talents in making the strongest manhattans that ever existed. It was all about the bitters. I am certain that that had a role in my mother's drinking issues as life moved forward. Every evening, the adults would gather to share about their day over his manhattans. Sometimes tempers would flare when someone believed another got more than they. I did not understand the heated discussions. I just knew it best to stay quiet and occupy myself elsewhere. I believe that my family's alcohol abuse and dysfunction prevented me from living life to the fullest.

My mother and I lived together in an apartment not far from my grandparents. I loved my mother though there were moments in life when we were distant from each other, even while living in the same house. My mother did take me to the art museum nearby and exposed me to a wide variety of music that I have enjoyed throughout my life. Our relationship improved later, when we lived nine hundred miles apart.

The happiest memory of my childhood was my six and a half years old birthday celebration. I do not know why we celebrated the half year, but it was a special event in my life. It was held at my grandparents' house. My mother had three brothers, so I remember several of my cousins being there. There were so many people. I received more presents than I got on my real birthday. The special bike that I had really been wanting…I got that, too.

I was born an Episcopalian; both of my parents were raised in the Episcopal church. I attended a private Episcopal school from kindergarten through third grade. We began each day with mass. The liturgy, music, and ritual of the service had a profound effect on me as a child. However, I did notice that only the boys were permitted to be acolytes. That's what I really wanted to do, so when I was at my grandparents in the summer, I would play church. I was an acolyte and carried a toilet plunger as the candle.

It was the summer between the fifth and sixth grade when we moved to Florida. My grandfather retired, so we all packed up and moved south. My mother and I lived with them for a short time until we found our own house. We moved to a house built in a community within an old orange grove. There were mostly boys on our street. This was perfect for me... lots of sports! We were all around the same age so I developed some pretty close friendships. I found myself gravitating to the boys. We rode our bikes together to and from school and enjoyed exploring the old orange grove where our housing development was being created. We chose teams and played dodgeball, flag football, and cleared an area on a vacant lot to play baseball. I was always the first to be chosen. I could throw a football better than any of the boys. The boy who lived across the street and I created our own lawn cutting business in the neighborhood. I really enjoyed those times.

When I was between ten and twelve, I discovered two girls on our street kissing and hugging each other in the orange grove a couple of times. This was a defining moment that began to reveal my sexuality. I was so jealous of their relationship!

Living in Florida gave me the opportunity to see my paternal grandparents from time to time. I cherished the letters my grandmother wrote to me in between visits.

My mother and I attended the neighborhood Episcopal church on Sundays. I enjoyed spending time with her there but the priest expected all children to leave for Sunday school during the sermon. One Sunday, he strongly "encouraged" me to do so right in front of the entire congregation. I was terribly embarrassed because he stopped to single me out and I refused to go. We never went back to that church again!

In my early teen years, I had become turned off by church, once again, thanks to the Presbyterian church we attended in Florida. The pastor appeared to focus on raising money for mission work in his native land and for material things around the church, but I never saw any results. It seemed hypocritical enough for me to refuse to go to my confirmation. We never went back to that church.

There were times in my early teen years when my mom's drinking her way to the bottom of a fifth of bourbon was more important to her than anything else, so I entertained myself with television and listened to records. I was too embarrassed for friends to know so I kept it to myself.

Even as a child, I recognized that my family was dysfunctional, so I looked to other families as role models. I watched as my friend's families invited others who might have been alone to spend holiday meals or for Sunday dinners with them. I watched when families had conversations with each other without endless arguing. I watched when families did things together that brought laughter and good memories that were shared over time and I took it all in. I was always grateful when a wise word was passed on to me in a moment of need. Later in life, my therapist would say that I "never learned to how to bond because no one in my family ever did it." God always put people in my path that I could learn the right way to do life. It gave me hope.

My last year of middle school, I was finally permitted to play on sports teams because they were established for girls that year. I played basketball, volleyball, softball, and ran track. But all sports stopped when I went to high school. My mom's drinking increased during my middle school years. She continued the pattern of drinking until she passed out. She was unavailable to me so when I started high school; sports were held at the end of the day. Mom resented having to drive me, so because I did not have transportation home after practice, I could not play.

I was sixteen when my mother, who had been in a relationship with a guy she had been seeing for a year and a half, became pregnant. When the man found out about the baby, he confessed he was married and left. My brother, though sixteen years younger, and I have a very special bond. I took care of him as a baby pretty much until he was two years old. We have a sweet relationship. He lives in another state now but is always ready to be here if I need him.

My feelings of same-sex attraction began intensifying during middle school and became even greater during high school. But this time in my life was wonderful, thanks to Susan. Susan was a new girl who came to my school in the ninth grade. I fell madly in love with her. We became very good friends! We wrote notes to each other every day in school and talked to each other after school on the phone. While she knew how I felt, we never discussed it and I could never act on it. I was too shy and reticent. Though she did not feel the same strong feelings I did, she was not scared away either. We just never talked about it.

The highlight of my high school years was seeing Susan every day until we moved in the middle of my senior year. We stayed good friends through high school and into our college years until she married a guy and had three kids.

We moved to the east coast of Florida and the culture in my new high school was different. I knew no one. The girls were all girly and the boys were only interested in having sex. I tried to deny my feelings of same-sex attraction and dated a guy there. We went to a drive-in movie and all he wanted to do was "make out." I was so uncomfortable, I never went out with him again. I felt like I did not belong.

Even though most of the parents of the students worked in the space program at Cape Canaveral, the school was rated on the surprisingly low end of the scale of academic achievement. Despite that, students did not just get passed through the system either. The oldest student was twenty-two years old. The school had a section in the library of first readers for those students who could not read. It also had a track for pregnant girls. These students were kept separate from the others. School was a big beach and surfing scene with much drinking and sex. The goal for most girls after high school was to get married and have children. There was no option to go to college.

I did have some successes in the new high school. I was the only one in my class that completed a vocabulary project successfully my senior year. My classmates were astonished. We were instructed to take one hundred vocabulary words, search magazines for them as used in sentences, cut out the sentences, and glue them to notecards. Fortunately, we did not have to provide our resources. I found ninety-five percent of them in *Playboy* magazine articles! They belonged to my uncles, of course. It was a happy moment for me in many ways.

My same-sex attraction continued through high school. It was difficult because I had no role models or anyone to talk about it with. The only girls I knew that were gay were athletes. Even though I loved playing sports, they were butch and rough, and I was not anything like them. I just could not make the connection. Where did I fit?

I graduated in 1968 and started college the following fall. I found myself in a relationship with a guy for two years, then it was over. He felt like I was "not into" the relationship so he moved on to someone else. Someone far more girly than I.

I was eighteen years old when my father and I were reconnected by my paternal grandmother. Life at home was not great and my grandmother knew I needed a better place to live. That is when I first met my stepmother. She was a wonderful caring woman and I came to really love her.

The summer of 1971, I moved back north to my "home" town. I was just shy of my twentieth birthday. The situation at my mother's home in Florida deteriorated even more. Having finished two years of college, I could see no future for us there. My mother and I strongly disagreed on how to raise my brother. I really wanted to get him out of that environment. It was difficult leaving him behind, but I had a plan. I was going to get a job so I could support both my brother and me. My paternal grandparents packed me up and moved me back. They thought it would be in my best interest to reconnect me with my father and stepmother.

My father offered to have me move in with them and I did so for a year. It gave me the opportunity to come to know my sister and two brothers. After my stepmother's death from a cerebral hemorrhage at the end of that first year, and my father's immediate remarriage, it became completely clear that the grass was only greener on my own. I moved into my first apartment! It was a second-floor apartment of an old house owned by an elderly German woman with heart issues. She and I became dear friends. Several years went by, and I had moved on to another place when I found out that she needed heart surgery. She was told that surgery would only increase her life by six more months if she made it through the surgery. If she did not have the surgery she would die in three weeks. She sought advice from me, asking, "what should I do?" It became a come to Jesus moment for me. This defining moment took me back to church after so many years. I answered that she needed to do what she thought best. She did have the surgery and made it through but died in the recovery room. To this day, I miss my Sweet Potato, with her round delicate face, crooked mouth smile, and German accent.

Then, in my mid-twenties, after having this and other challenging experiences, I came back to the Episcopal church. This became a place of spiritual renewal and strengthening which prepared me for more challenges ahead—the death of a close friend, the death of my half-brother who died in a freak accident and coming to terms with my sexuality. These brought me back to God as I tried to make sense of them.

Once on my own, my plan was to work, make something of myself, and raise enough money to support my youngest brother took much longer than I thought. After seeking advice from a lawyer friend, and talking with Social Services, the possibility of my being able to take custody of my brother became clearly non-existent. It was so disappointing. He has grown to be an amazing man despite it all. Our mother seemed to learn from my growing up and did things differently. Better.

In my twenties, it was still difficult to keep hearing the societal expectations that I should do what is right and get married and have children. So, I gave in to the expectations and in 1973, and I married a very handsome guy that shared similar interests. We liked to camp, canoe, and all kinds of sports. He seemed like a nice guy and I really liked him, but the marriage was rocky and it did not last. I tried to be who I thought I was supposed to be. I had not seen how selfish and self-centered he was. He took a job as a caseworker and fell for a co-worker who pursued him. It was over.

In my late twenties, one of my priests at the time who was coaching my spiritual journey, introduced me to Henri Nouwen's book, *Reaching Out*. She actually threw it at me, saying, "Here read this." Through the message in this book, I learned of the spiritually loving concept of hospitality and honoring the sacred space that is present between us, a perspective that has been life altering for me. I always strive to acknowledge and honor the space that lies between myself and others as sacred and I constantly search for ways, the simple basic ways, to honor that sacred space in every encounter. I have learned to set my boundaries when that space is not honored.

It was not until I met and moved in with another guy in my early thirties that I began to accept the fact that I was a lesbian. He figured it out along the way and helped me to embrace who I really was. I remember him taking me to a movie about a lesbian, *Personal Best*. He understood me and did everything he could to support me as I learned to accept myself. He encouraged me to pursue a relationship with a woman. For more than thirty years now, we have stayed connected with birthday wishes.

I wanted to share my new journey with the priest who had been my spiritual director. It seemed like the best place to share my inner life. I had been in the closet for so long. Her response surprised me. She said, "I don't need to know." So once again, I walled myself back up to being open about my same-sex attraction.

Shortly after that time, I met a woman that I was attracted to and I could not deny it. I had to be hit over the head with a brick, so to speak, but I went for it. We lived together for a year. The thrill of bringing someone "out" was over by then for her and she moved on. I moved out and bought my own house.

As I entered deeper into the LGBTQ community, I began to make more and more friends. I met professional women just like me. I began to feel more comfortable with my true self and life. While I did not date much, I was good at "assessing" women without dating them.

I finally came out to my family on my thirty-fourth birthday. I remembered the jokes made at the expense of the LGBTQ people while I was growing up, I swallowed hard, wrote each family member a letter and hand delivered it that day. That night, I went to dinner with good friends, my family of choice. These were the people who had come to know me and love me no matter what. We went to celebrate my life, which now felt like a breath of fresh air.

The responses to my coming out were a mixed bag. Only one brother called that night. On my voice messaging was his voice telling me that he loved me. The rest were silent in varying ways. A few days later, I went to dinner with my father and second stepmother. From them, I got a long list of the things I was not allowed to do going forward when around the family: bringing another gay person home for family gatherings was prohibited, anyone I was dating was not welcome, no longer being allowed to babysit my nieces or nephew, nor be alone with them, no auntie sleep-overs! Blah, blah, blah. Coming out to my family had its challenges.

I have been in my present place of worship for the last thirty years. It has become a place where I can have an impact on changing attitudes and challenging other lesbians to live a fuller life. I have a quiet, caring nature, and feminine qualities and appearance. Coming out in my mid-thirties, I found that this Episcopal parish was the perfect church home for me. On the very first visit, the rector stood in front of the church after services and told the congregation he was going downtown that afternoon to the Inner Harbor, to march in the very first gay pride march in Baltimore. He made it clear he was not going as a representative of the church, but instead felt he personally needed to give his support to gay and lesbian people. My mouth dropped. I could not believe my ears. Serendipity? Looking back, this moment was a calling.

As I began to live my life fully, get involved, and meet people, I watched the stereotypic view of homosexuality and "lifestyle" (a term which has always made me laugh because I live my life more morally and ethically straight than most "straight" people) by fellow congregants shift to enlightened understanding and then acceptance. Love grew as families with gay children engaged me in conversation and they became more accepting and loving of each other. This is the church where I have chosen to raise my children. I want them to see and know the difference love makes.

Eight years later, in my early forties, a friend of mine who had just finished seminary invited me to an event that changed my life. I had attended many social gatherings she and her partner coordinated in the past. This time was different. It was through them that I met my beloved. I was invited to their Halloween party and was not expecting to go alone but the woman I had been dating was very self-centered and said she "had made other plans." So, I went alone. There, a woman dressed as road kill, complete with a fake dead rat on her shoulder, spent most of the night conversing with me. I politely responded. Tess had just gotten out of a relationship with someone who had moved to Florida and then found someone else. Apparently, Tess "fell head over heels" for me that night. She later recanted how she had called two of her best friends after the party saying that she had found the perfect person for her, saying "this is the one."

After weeks of asking, I finally consented to our first date. I had ended the relationship with the woman I was dating and decided to explore again. Our first date was to see the movie *The Piano*. We met at the theater and parted and went our separate ways. There was not much opportunity for conversation. The movie was so heavy we did not know what to say to each other afterwards. Much later, this night became a humorous story to tell.

Tess continued to pursue me. We talked on the phone at night for hours, and a few months after our first date, I said yes to another. We went for coffee before our movie, "Mrs. Doubtfire." Tess really made me laugh. Now, people had always commented to me that they never see me smile. Sitting across from her as we drank our coffee, I knew I was in so much trouble. She made me laugh. Deep belly-shaking laughter. We had a lovely time.

As we spent more time together, I realized I knew happiness when I was with her. I smiled all the time. My life was fuller, and our relationship grew stronger. But, my past relationships had made me very hesitant to move into another relationship, so I took it very slowly. I was honest with Tess. If it was going to work I decided I was going to be completely honest and she would have to accept me as I am. And my dog. And she did!

I had fallen deeply in love with her and love kept growing. In February 1994, we knew that this was it. In August, I moved into Tess's house. Crime was increasing in the neighborhood where my home was located in the city. It was safer out in the country. In September, we shopped for rings and spoke our words of commitment to one another. I was so happy in the life that Tess and I were creating together. We both were. In June 1996, we bought a house together—a four-bedroom, two-and-a-half-bath, 2,300-square-foot house! So you need to fill it, right?

As our love grew, so did our desire to have a family and we began the process. After all, we now had a big house to fill and share! Tess had always wanted to have children and I had always wanted to adopt. I was in my late forties by then, so Tess, just turning forty, was the likely candidate to give birth. For two years, Tess tried to get pregnant without success. We discovered a uterine condition that prevented pregnancy from taking hold and that made it necessary for Tess to have a hysterectomy.

We decided it best to take a year to grieve. Since childhood, I have always been close to the idea of adoption. It always bothered me to know there were kids in the world who did not have parents. I suggested that we adopt. A year later the adoption process began.

At the time, adoption for a lesbian couple was very difficult. Domestic adoption in the United States was forbidden. China would permit you to adopt if you would sign a form declaring your heterosexuality. Tess was not willing to discount our relationship by lying about it. We had heard from friends that one specific adoption agency would permit a single parent adoption from a Latin American country. The partner would be identified as a "roommate." We agreed that Tess would do the single parent adoption and the process began. The home study was very in-depth on both of us, being psychologically evaluated as to whether we each would be a good parent, making sure our families were functionally normal people, being fingerprinted and investigated on the local, state, and federal levels. It took about a year from beginning to end. In late 2000, we brought our first daughter home to a welcoming committee of family and close friends at the airport and then a baby shower the next day with huge number of loving, supportive, excited-for-us people I have ever seen at a baby shower.

Love in our home only grew. We liked being moms and wanted to share our love even more. We decided to adopt again. We left it to God whether we got a girl or boy as a referral. We figured that in pregnancy, you cannot order a boy or girl so why do that now. We prayed this time, as we did the first, for the right baby spirit to come to us. Our second daughter came home in 2003. Each of our daughters arrived to band of family and friends waiting to greet them in the airport and welcome them home.

Even though the girls were adopted in their birth country, the United States required a second court adoption process in the U.S. before it became final. In January 2004, we completed the second adoption here in the U.S. with Tess legally becoming their momma. A second parent adoption could be done at the same time, so I became their legal second parent, otherwise known as mommy. I would legally be the girls' second mom. Prior to this court date, I had to go through an extensive home study of my own where I was psychologically evaluated again, and fingerprinted for investigation on the local, state, and federal levels. We also had to have our home inspected by a fire marshal for hazards and we had follow-up visits for six months after the adoption by a social worker.

What would it be like if all parents had to go through a "home study" evaluation process determining if they would be "fit" parents before having children?

Life was happy. Good. Loving. Friends and family were excited for us and supportive of us and the girls.

In the spring of 2006, Tess experienced pain down her right arm with tingling in her hand and slight pain across the top of her chest on the right. The doctor ordered x-rays. A herniated cervical disc was diagnosed. And, although he was not concerned, as a precaution, the doctor ordered an MRI of her chest because of a "blip" to the right of her sternum. Then, came more tests from specialists and the diagnosis. Cancer. It was called lung cancer even though the site was in a lymph node under her sternum and her lungs were clear. Our life was turned upside down. Why us? We were good people.

Radiation and chemotherapy followed. Friends, family, and co-workers surrounded us with their love, prayers, encouragement, and help. We sought a second opinion for treatment. The tumor shrank considerably. For a few months, it seemed to have gone away. Then, it was clear, growth was happening again. An aggressive second round of chemotherapy began. It depleted Tess to a poor quality of life very quickly. The decision to stop the chemo was made to help make her remaining days the best they could be. Her quality of life was primary. Tess entered hospice at home in September of 2007. She was not expected to live past Halloween, certainly not Thanksgiving. Well, Tess still had things to do and celebrate so she didn't die when expected.

What does one do when you don't die when you are supposed to? You go to Disney World! We had already begun to save the money to take the girls to Disney. Tess was still committed to make that happen. In March of 2007, thanks to the Dream Foundation, what we saved, family and friends, and hospice, we made the trip with the girls' godparents in tow to help out. We discovered friends of ours were there the same week and staying close to us sharing in the fun. Hospice care in Orlando was on call if we needed them and came periodically to check on Tess. It was so important to Tess to experience the girls in Disney. She soldiered through with a powered wheel chair and oxygen portable concentrator, spending six out of the seven days we were in the various Disney parks not missing a beat.

But, there was more to do. Tess was determined to celebrate her fiftieth birthday in April. By then, she was declining and beginning to leave us. A huge gathering of friends, family, coworkers, the girls' teachers and her oncologist came to celebrate her. It was a beautiful warm, sunny day filled with Tess stories, laughter, photos, a pie in the face.

Hospice let us know one Friday in mid-May it would be soon. She was close. Family arrived from out of state. All day on Saturday family and close friends stopped by to say goodbye. She woke that day alert, by noon had slipped into unconsciousness. She passed away shortly before midnight. The girls had come into our room to lay in our bed to sleep. Literally the moment they slipped into sleep, Tess let go of her last breath as the Brad Paisley and Dolly Parton song "When I Get Where I'm Going" played in the background. I was in bed with her holding her. Her oncologist had come to be with her, holding her hand. She got the perfect peaceful ending she wanted.

Tess, my beloved, my wife, my best friend has had a profound effect on my life. She loved me unconditionally, supported me and inspired me. She always encouraged me to live fully. She allowed me to love her and received that love completely. It is through that love that I came to know the love of God for the first time.

The loss of Tess has been immense, and she leaves a legacy behind. I never dreamed I would have kids until I met Tess. We created a beautiful family together. I never imagined that I would be raising our kids without her.

I am left with beautiful memories...some are quite humorous. I remember being outed by our children when they were quite young. We were out in public settings and our girls would call each of us "mom." So much for living under the radar. People would do a double take but nothing more. I never really had to explain sexuality to them until they were in middle school. They knew they had two moms. It was normal. They knew a loving caring environment...more than some of their friends at times. Because they both attend Catholic school, when the discussion of homosexuality came up I simply reminded them they have an embodied experience different than what they were being told because they have two moms.

Now that they are in their teens, they understand the hypocrisy. They both have friends who already know they identify as gay or lesbian and they are there for them, love them, and support them. I do still have conversations with them around sexuality as life's situations bring it forth.

While I don't wish being gay on anyone, because of the discrimination, I would not change being lesbian for anything because of the absolute richness of people and experiences it has brought to my life. The gifts that it has brought to me, not only in terms of people, but what is important in life, has changed me. I have learned some very important lessons. If I had known what I know now, I would have been bolder and probably would have come out much earlier, in high school.

I feel fortunate that I haven't experienced as much discrimination as others have. All instances were mostly "minor" with one huge, life-pervading exception after Tess's passing. I have had guys pat their crotches saying they "have just what I need." In my family, there have been rules and limitations in being around my nieces and nephews. I have also been criticized by those in a gay religious organization for not being "out" in an "in your face" way. That's just not consistent with who I am. Then, there were the gay jokes or snickers in my presence during conversations.

Some of the worst discrimination experiences were when Tess had her hysterectomy and then, my experience of the estate laws after her death. During her hysterectomy, I waited in the waiting room while she was in recovery. The doctor had come immediately after surgery to tell me she had done well. It was hours past the time she should have been in her room and she was not. When I sought information from the recovery room, all they would say was she was still there. Fortuitously, I ran into the hospital chaplain, someone I knew. She went to talk to the nurse and returned with the reason. Tess's breathing kept stopping as she slept. They were concerned and were watching her closely. When I heard this I related, "Of course! She has sleep apnea." When that information was relayed back to the recovery room by the chaplain, they were all too happy to put her in a room and have me sit by her side to nudge her to remind her to breathe.

The most pervading and impactful discrimination came after Tess's death. She died before gay marriage became legal, granting the same rights of heterosexual couples to gay couples. As I sat going through the will process at the register of wills office it became shockingly clear to me the discrimination I was experiencing, things we worked hard to achieve and money the girls would no longer have available to them. I prayed the state would spend the tidy sum wisely. HA! Had I invested what I had to pay the state in estate tax, my daughters would have their college education paid for. Really!!! Even the folks at the register of wills became upset, declaring this was not right and kept apologizing. I simply thanked them and suggested that for the sake of other kids of gay couples in our county, when the gay rights bill came before the state legislature, they speak their discomfort with what they now saw as unfair. I, also, seem to be unable to receive Tess's social security benefits despite our fourteen and a half years together, to continue to provide for the girls past their eighteenth birthdays. If I were straight, I would have it for the remainder of my life.

Professionally, in my acupuncture practice early on, I had a patient who I treated for a short time that stopped coming when she heard I was a lesbian. As a rule, I usually avoid speaking about my personal life to my patients. This one patient asked directly if my deceased beloved was a woman. I swallowed hard and answered honestly. I never saw her after that. Later, in a conversation with her husband, he indicated that she felt uncomfortable with me. I asked why, had I done something to invoke this feeling from her. He shared that she had been sexually abused by her mother.

I have learned in life that each person needs to "live and be" every moment of their lives. Surround yourself with created family; people who love you unconditionally, support you, and encourage you to risk being the best you can be. Always remember *love* is a verb not just a feeling. Seek out those who love you and who you can trust and feel safe with, those who will not judge you. Be with people who want to be with you, laugh with you, share time with you, and allow you to be you. Be with those who want the best for you and are willing to kick your butt when necessary. Everyone needs a support team. LOVE...give it and receive it. Find ways to serve others. And, by all means...LAUGH!

I have hope for the future. For the girls, I hope for them to be strong, self-confident, independent, financially abundant, and loving women. I hope that they will come to know strong bonding love in their relationships and that they will have their own children, by whatever means they choose. And, I hope that they will stay close to God.

For myself, I desire to be in a loving relationship again, to continue to grow as a person, to LIVE again. Losing Tess has been very painful. Not only was she the love of my life but she was also the connection to our family and friends. Many of them left my life when she died. Tess's family stopped coming around though I am still close to her mom. For a long time, her family did not include us in family events. We were just starting to feel connected to them. Now, they are gone. Life has felt empty without them.

My daughters are also feeling the heavy burden of loss. Not only do they miss their momma, but they feel abandoned by so many family and friends. Our home is no longer filled with the laughter of those who used to be close to us.

I do have moments, I am finding that I really do not know what to hope for. I am praying but it appears that nothing seems to be working out. I still am highly involved in my church, but my faith is waning. My desire is to raise my children in a home of faith and love. So, I work at gratefulness.

Life can be a challenge, but love is the anecdote to the challenges. With love— God's love, friends' love, and family love—anything is possible. Live in gratitude…every moment; make memories, and pass love on.

*Laura is a healer and is working as a licensed acupuncturist and a Reiki Master in her private practice. She lives in the northeast with her two beautiful girls. She*

*Laura*

*holds degrees in Laboratory Technology, BS in Microbiology, and a Masters in Acupuncture.*

# *Henry*

## Chapter 11

*Henry's love of film started when he was very young. When it became time for him to commit himself to his passion, he came to America to pursue a master's in film. His films are an outward expression of the deepest part of him. They speak about his life experience—his childhood memories, the influences of his Asian culture, and his greatest fears.*

### *Henry's Story*

I do not have many happy memories of my childhood. Our family was very poor when I was young. I was an only child in a very conservative family in a small city in Asia. My relationship with my parents was polite. The culture is much more reserved, so I never remember having any physical affection, hugs or kisses, never an "I love you." This, too, is very cultural so it was never something that I missed. My parents did hold my hand as a young child to keep me safe. Safety is primary in my culture.

Because of the sense of lack in our city, there was no sense of community. There was a pervasive fear that someone would take the little that you had. That meant that there were no community gatherings, opportunities for team sports, or any type of group activities for children. Everyone kept to themselves. I engaged in solitary activities and learned to play the violin and piano and learned to paint.

One of the benefits of employment in my city was that the employer is responsible for providing a place for all employees to live. We lived in a small apartment provided by my mother's job. When the building was torn down, we moved to a community of homes built around a courtyard but there was still no connection with the neighbors.

I was raised in an area of Asia where religion was not as present as it is in America. Most people in my area were atheist. I learned later to have faith in my art, myself, and my dream as an artist and filmmaker.

My parents always valued higher education. I remember my father going to America to pursue his PhD degree when I was six years old. It was a big deal to go to study there and I knew of no other parents that did that. He was gone for three years though it felt like six or seven to me. After he left for America, it was just me and my mother, so she had the most influence in my life.

My father's absence caused me to start to feel isolated for the first time. I have a vivid memory of my mother deciding that she needed to go to shopping with her friend one afternoon instead of hanging out with me. I remember running after her bike in hope that she would not go. It's funny to think about it now because I cannot recall at all the moment she left Asia to join my father in America for a year, but I could remember the afternoon she went shopping without me.

After my mother left, I lived with my paternal grandparents. They were elderly and focused on keeping me safe during this time. I had a few friends but rarely played with them. Most of my time was spent with my grandparents. My memories of childhood at this age were very practical ones. How much homework did I need to do? What did I need to learn? I felt isolated and alone most of the time. I don't remember too much sadness, it was just life.

My first impression of America was when my parents returned. They came bearing gifts. I couldn't wait to open the salmon from the "deep ocean." This was a big deal. My parents wanted to have a gathering of their relatives to share the salmon from the "deep ocean" and to celebrate their return so I was forced to wait. I will never forget my disappointment when the fish was finally served. It tasted horrible. The "liquid chocolate" (chocolate syrup) was strange and new but much tastier. This started my fantasy about America.

Adolescence became very challenging for me. When I entered middle school, I started to experience same-sex attraction. Gay jokes were always somewhat popular in Asia, as a way to emasculate and de-humanize a man. This made me feel very uncomfortable. I remember thinking that one student was very handsome. I guess that probably was my first awakening of my sexual orientation. I never talked with that person, so nothing more happened. It was not until much later that I began to understand what I was experiencing.

The saving grace of this time was that my dream of becoming a filmmaker began to take root in my heart. It gave me hope for my future. I watched and collected as many movies as possible. I started reading film magazines that spoke about many of the films from America. This had a major impact on me and out of that developed a desire to go west.

But the older I got (as much as I tried to hide it), my authentic-self began to emerge, and people noticed me. Discrimination was everywhere. In high school, there was a bully who would wait outside of my class every day just so he could call me "freak" in front of everyone. I guess he sensed that I was "different." I was so afraid, I never had the courage to even look in his eyes to know what he looked like. Going to school every day was terrifying for me.

The concept of being an Asian gay man in our homophobic and conservative small city was very difficult. First, I really didn't totally understand it myself and there was no one I could talk to about it. The little information I did have of the homosexual life, I found on the internet. I remember feeling like a "freak" and a "second class person" growing up. I lived in constant fear and hid who I was.

The increased academic pressure in high school helped to divert some of the attention from me. High school is all about preparing for the SAT. If you are successful in high school, you are set for life. Everything is taught with this test in mind. There was no room for creativity…only book knowledge (film was not part of the curriculum). The school system set the goals for each person's life. Students were required to choose one of two tracks: science (which included biology, physics and chemistry) and literature (which included history, politics, and geology). Everyone learned English, math, and our native language. In my culture, the score on the SAT is a major life event. It determines your future success.

Because I am an only child, my parents had very severe expectations for me. They had their own ideas for the person they wanted me to become. My parents wanted me to be a scientist or doctor since they are both in the field of science. My father is a biologist and my mother a nurse. I chose the science route to appease them. I completed my high school years successfully.

My passion to be a filmmaker continued to grow so when it came time to choose a college, I chose one that had a directing major. My parents thought I was joking when I informed them of my decision. When they realized that I was serious they became angry and started to pressure me to choose a different course of study. I insisted and began a hunger strike to convince them. They decided that they would take me to see an artist in a large city in Asia in hopes that he would change my mind. He informed me that I didn't have sufficient talent to be successful in the directing major and that I should listen to my parents. I stood firm and went forward with my choice, developing in my greatest passion…film.

While in college, I developed a close relationship with a Frenchman who was doing an exchange study in economics in the city where I was attending college. He was introduced to me by one of my good friends. I had never met a gay person before. He told me about his life as a gay man and the struggles he had encountered—not being accepted by others and not accepting himself. It was something I never had the opportunity to talk about with anyone before. We hung out together for about three months, going to dinner, traveling, and going to parties. We partied a lot. I was very attracted to him, related to him deeply, and I started to build a fantasy around how "we needed to be together to save each other." We had some very deep conversations, so he knew of the fantasy that I projected on him. However, he was a very reserved and troubled person, so we never got together. If he did not want to be reached, he would just disappear. It hurt me deeply because I felt humiliated after offering myself to someone completely, then getting rejected. I have grown considerably from that experience. I understand that most of my "savior" complex is not much related to that person himself but to the social, racial, and life history of my formation. I cannot escape it. It took me years to understand that I do not need him or anyone to "save" me. We have remained friends and talk every six months. It is a weird relationship and he understands he has power over me. I understand that also. It's quite poisonous for me but I am curious to see what is next. I went to Paris to see him again two years after he left Asia.

After completing my college degree in Asia in directing, I came to America to complete a master's in film and make movies. The inspiration of my films continues to be from my own personal experiences. One of my first films is about a gay man who has had a one-night stand and the loss he feels afterwards. This film has deeply touched hearts and has been played at film festivals all around the world. Slowly, I am being recognized as an artist and filmmaker. This was all I ever wanted… to live that dream.

## Henry

It wasn't until I came to America that I started to understand another layer of my identity. It was a mind-blowing experience for me to jump from the most conservative culture right into the most liberal of environments. Then slowly, I started to understand that the problems I have had within myself were from growing up in an environment that is hostile toward who I am. I would not and could not say I have become a new person since I came to America, but on some level my education has given me a way to see the world, myself, and to express my voice. The geographical change, from a small city in Asia to America, was my chance to move into a "new life." But, of course, life is a long journey to slowly understand and create myself.

I was twenty-two when I first told someone that I was gay. It was one of my classmates. It was not much of a decision. I basically thought, okay this is my new life, and this is what I am going to do. It was not planned, and I cannot remember what I said. I didn't have a big moment or feeling after telling the person. I really think many people had just figured it out about me. It was a gradual process for me to agree with them. I didn't really need to tell a lot of people.

I still have not come out to my family, yet. I don't think my parents would understand me at all. I believe it would be the end of our relationship. I have no friends or relatives in Asia that are gay. No one would even talk about it there.

I have never really dated anyone before. I have very high expectations about what a loving relationship should be. Part of this, I believe, is because of my lack of experience. My concept of love is naive and in some ways like Disney fantasies in their "prince and princess" movies. Hopefully my expectation is not too unrealistically high. Over the years, I am beginning to understand myself slightly better. I think I would prefer to wait for a relationship that is mutual…where we both deserve each other.

I do have many supportive friends here in America. One of the biggest influences in my life has been my mentor. She has helped me to find my voice autobiographically as a filmmaker. It has given me faith in my art, myself, and my dream as an artist and filmmaker.

I have learned a few lessons over the years. The first lesson has been to accept myself as a gay man. The second is to accept myself as an Asian gay man. To understand the American freedom and gay culture is difficult. Freedom is not only limited by sexual orientation but also racism. It is important for me to understand myself as I live in a society that doesn't provide me with examples of people like me.

I have no words of advice for others coming out. I am still working out the details of that myself. Give me another thirty years to come up with my first words of wisdom. It is my hope that my films will speak. If someone feels touched or feels that there are people in the world just like them because of my films, that's great. I am just going to continue making my films and creating my voice as an Asian LGBTQ artist filmmaker.

# Henry

*Henry has been in America making films for five years. His heartfelt movies are autobiographical in nature; an expression of his life as an Asian gay man. It is his hope to stay and continue his career.*

# Luca

## Chapter 12

*Luca was raised in a very small town in the deep south. The younger of two sons, he could not have been any more different from his brother. His brother was extremely masculine, very bright, played sports, hunted, fished, and was very outgoing, much like his father. Luca wasn't. He was quieter and was not interested in sports, hunting or fishing in the least. Compared to his brother and father, he was a "sissy" and he felt it extremely difficult to fit in. His mother seemed to understand him well, so he clung to her.*

### Luca's Story

We were not the type of family that had dinner together at the end of the day. My father worked full-time and went to law school at night. My mother taught language arts and reading at the local middle school. My brother was always very busy with sports. I played sports for a while also but quit after not being successful at something that I didn't enjoy. I felt different. I just could not find my place.

My mother claims that she knew I was gay when I was three years old. One of *my* earliest memories was wanting to wear pink shoes and pink shirts to first grade. My mother handled the request well. She bought them for me and my brother took the responsibility of trying to protect me from the teasing that I received. When the teasing got to be too much he took a sharpie and drew a Nike symbol on my new shoes in hopes that that would remedy the situation. He wouldn't let anyone make fun of me... although that didn't stop him at times.

As I got a little older, it became more and more difficult for me to be myself. I wasn't even sure of who I was. I was supposed to be an athlete like my brother, but I had more of an interest in the arts. I liked theater and music, books, movies, going to the pool, and playing with friends. My mother was a theater major and trained me to do acting. I entered the gifted program in school for talent, not brains. My brother, of course, got in for brains. I felt safe with him so I often followed him around, whether he liked it or not. He was my protector in a way, and he tolerated this well... most of the time.

My neighborhood was a great place to grow up. There was always something going on and friends to play with. But at age eleven, things took a drastic turn when my family moved out of the neighborhood. My mom desired to build a house and have a horse farm.

When my family moved, I felt extremely isolated. I didn't know any of my neighbors. We lived on twenty acres of land with very few houses in sight. I missed my old friends terribly and was very angry at my parents for making me move. It was too many changes to deal with. So, we lived on a beautiful horse farm which taught me more about hard work than I ever cared to learn. I was not a big fan, but it soon became home.

The backward ways of the culture in our small town made it very difficult for me. I was entering my adolescence when we moved. My brother was in high school and was not nearly as affected because he had friends who could drive. He was gone a lot of the time which made me feel even more isolated. My middle school years were very gray. I stopped playing sports, gained weight and had terrible acne. I wanted to be smarter than I was and couldn't make as good of grades as I wanted. Life was a real struggle.

It was during this time that I started to notice men's bodies. It started with my dad. I found my attraction toward the same sex very hard to deal with. I did not feel right in my own skin. I started behaving irrationally because this scared me.

When I was fourteen, my brother saw pictures I had printed off the Internet of very attractive men in their underwear. He questioned it, but I explained to him that I used it as motivation to work out so I could look like them. I was trying to lose the weight that I had gained from not playing sports. I think that my brother knew about me but was more worried about what would happen if the word got out. I found out later that he constantly told people, "We don't know if he is gay for sure, so let's leave it alone."

My mother caught me looking at gay porn when I was fifteen. She asked me, "Are you sexually attracted to men?" I didn't answer. I cried my way out of it. I believe that my mother would have been fine if I had come out then. However, I seriously worried that if I came out, she would somehow get fired from her teaching job. Small towns do things like this and try to cover it up with something else.

When I entered high school, things began to turn around. I started playing soccer again and had friends that I could talk to. It was helpful that my brother was a senior and could drive me to school. I enjoyed being in school with his class because I had known his friends for many years.

Being raised in the church helped in many ways. Though my brother and I were both baptized Episcopalian, when my family moved, we were invited to attend a Methodist church. It became our church. I was always involved there and made the choice to accept Jesus Christ as my Lord and Savior at age fifteen. I attended the youth group at church and the Fellowship of Christian Athletes at my high school. God became very real to me at age sixteen. Having a relationship with Him was special.

Life became much more difficult at school after my brother graduated. I was a sophomore and missed having he and his friends around. The legacy he left behind was hard to follow, too. I felt like I was supposed to live up to his athleticism and academics, and I was constantly feeling that I was never good enough.

I was successful in high school but not happy. I was different, and this became more and more obvious. Persecution was real and rose to a whole new level during this time. I grew up in the roots of racism and homophobia, along with hunting, guns, and rednecks. Everything inappropriate was said to me and I cried often. Teenagers can be especially cruel.

Church had always been a very safe place for me but persecution began to move into every area of my life. FCA camp became especially difficult for me one summer. I thought it was nice that many "masculine" guys at these events were nice to me and this allowed me to get away from being a "sissy boy" in my small southern town. When you were expected to be tough, masculine, an athlete, and a farmer, being a "sissy boy" was unacceptable.

I was a very strong Christian when I was sixteen, and enjoyed attending a Christian camp for a few days each summer. It was usually hard for me to feel like I fit in with the masculine guys there, but I felt like I was doing pretty well at camp this particular year until one night. My counselor asked that I come to talk to him privately. I really didn't think much of it and went to meet with him. He said he needed to just flat out ask me if anyone had ever talked to me about homosexuality. I was speechless. This was the last thing I thought he would ask. I gave a phony smile and explained that there was nothing for him to be concerned about. He then suggested that I talk with a different counselor. He took me to meet the new counselor shortly after our conversation. I recognized him and found him to be somewhat feminine. Everyone at the camp believed he was gay, but apparently, after he gave his life to Christ, he was no longer gay. Maybe they hoped the same would happen to me. This really upset me.

It seemed like people were always trying to tell me I was gay long before I could figure it out for myself. There were plenty of Bible thumpers in my hometown who told me how wrong homosexuality was; people who wanted to "out" me in a cruel way. When I could finally admit that I did have these feelings, it was hard to know what to think. Some people thought that I could still be straight because I was such a "ladies' man." Some thought I could just ignore how I was feeling and not commit the sin of living a homosexual lifestyle.

Adolescence is a very confusing time for everyone. When I say that teenagers don't know themselves, I mean that there is a lot of eccentric behavior. Teens do things that don't make sense because they don't know who they are. I observed this even in my closest friends. My best friend was constantly calling me "gay" behind my back, even though he had a gay uncle that he got along well with. His older sister, also, made some crude comments towards me and said that I was a girl, when in fact she was a major tomboy who later came out as a lesbian. One of my best girlfriends also had gay uncles that she liked, yet she still made some rude comments to me that were hurtful. As we have grown older and become adults, so have our views on homosexuality. I still consider all three of these people my friends. They have become some of my biggest supporters, just like I am theirs.

People often respond negatively to the gay community out of their misconceptions. In high school, I had a friend who was also a strong Christian like myself, who happened to have a lesbian mother. People were very mean to her because of this and told her that she dressed like a "dyke." It upset her and she is not even a lesbian. Gay parents do not make gay babies. My own parents thought I wanted to be a girl during my teenage years and told the doctors that I seemed to have a gender identity disorder. This was not the case. I hung around girls a lot more because I was much more comfortable with them.

In December 2001, I stayed home from school one morning as I had done multiple times to avoid persecution. This time, my dad was tired of my behavior and felt the need to talk to me about it. I tried explaining to him that it was very hard for me to go to school because of the pressure I was always feeling. I told him that I just did not seem to be like most guys. He reminded me that I was okay. He was a lawyer who represented juvenile delinquents, drug users, fathers of teenage pregnancies, etc. So, I looked pretty good to him. Even though I didn't drink or do drugs or have premarital sex, I still felt like I was a "bad" kid for skipping school. I tried to tell my dad that on top of everything else, I was tired of being called "gay" or a "faggot" at school. He simply responded with, "But you're not." And that was that. I didn't have any room left to say anything. When you're sixteen years old, living in a small town, and living under your parents' roof, you are forced to go with what they say.

A similar experience happened when my mother encouraged me to see a counselor the same year. I felt like the counselor was trying to upset me about being gay. This was contrary to what my mother had in mind. My mother's purpose for the counseling was to help me learn to love myself for who I am. She never tried to make me feel bad about being gay.

It was easy to misinterpret the messages that I got from people. When my brother's friend from college came out after they graduated, I remember talking to my dad about him. My dad asked me, "Do his friends still talk to him?" This scared me. In my mind, I thought, "Oh, my gosh. My dad thinks that he is no longer a person who deserves to have friends. He would definitely never accept me." I took this way too seriously. All my dad was asking was, "Were people willing to accept the friend for who he is?" It is not uncommon for me to take things personally or be very sensitive to anything resembling gay issues.

Being bullied is a very painful experience as a young gay person. The suicide rate for LGBTQ teens is extremely high. At one time, I considered suicide because I was miserable as a teenager and felt so alone. I didn't know any gay people that I could talk to. They were supposed to be evil. My faith in God is what helped me not give up on my life.

When I was twenty-four, my mom finally felt the need to talk to me about it directly. A good friend had shared with her about her own son coming out. My mom came home and started a conversation that I was not prepared for so I avoided it.

Over the next few months, I went through my first same-sex relationship. It went badly, and the guy chose his addiction over me. I was crushed and since I hadn't confessed my true sexuality to my parents, I couldn't talk to them about it. They knew that I was hurting, but I couldn't tell them why. My mom, having been tired of my aloof and hostile behavior, finally questioned me about everything a few months later and I was finally honest. She told me to talk to my dad, and that he would be fine, too. This was a huge relief.

My dad was a conservative republican. I thought that he would maybe drop dead the day he knew for sure that he had a gay son. Instead, he was very compassionate. He seemed to understand that people "choose to be gay as much as they choose their own skin color." I couldn't believe how much he understood me. Coming out to my dad brought us so much closer. There had been a rift in our relationship since I was a teenager. I was so grateful that my dad and I reconciled our relationship because he died a year later.

My family was so supportive of me when I came out. My parents had said that they had "the talk" prepared since I was young. It was a relief. My dad wanted to announce it to his family at my grandmother's 80th birthday party. I could see how supportive he was, but I told him not to steal my grandma's thunder. They heard about it later.

My extended family use to believe that being gay was horrible. One of my cousins had married a man when I was very young who turned out to be gay. I don't remember this man very well. Two years into their marriage, he was unfaithful to her with a man. She was tested for AIDS and they divorced. They learned about me later and have been very accepting.

I do have to say that the biggest influence on my life has been my brother. When I came out, he told me how proud he was of me. He has always tried to protect me from the derogatory remarks that people made about me. I know he had a hard time understanding gay people when he was younger, but he always stood by me. He never looked at people as gay or straight. He was nice to everyone. He befriended the one guy in his high school class that everyone suspected was gay and came out after their graduation. In college, one of his best friends in his fraternity was openly gay. My brother was once very conservative in his political beliefs, but still didn't discriminate against the LGBTQ community. These conservative views did change after he served in the military in Iraq. He has always been a safe place for me to go and was one of the first people to whom I confessed that I was experiencing same-sex attraction. I've always been proud to call him my brother.

I have heard of many people coming out over the years. As far as my friends are concerned, one of my best friend's sister came out as a lesbian, after high school. Another childhood friend came out in high school. I went to a small liberal arts Christian college where no one could come out while attending, but some people did later. Several people from my home church came out, just not while attending it. They each kept the secret for a long time.

Going to my ten-year high school reunion was a great turning point for me. I was out and proud and some of the people who gave me a hard time have done a complete 180 degrees. They were much nicer and very supportive.

I wish I could control it, but it matters what people think of me. If they are afraid of me, it is usually because they don't know me or anyone else that might be gay. I was hired to work with a woman once for my aunt's business. My aunt explained to the woman ahead of time that I was gay. Apparently, she was very hesitant to work with me but still gave me a chance, and we ended up being great friends. She still calls me to connect and we haven't worked together in over five years.

I have experienced some discrimination in my professional life because of my sexual orientation. I applied for a teaching position in my hometown and later learned that I did not get the job because of my sexuality, even though I was the most qualified. Hopefully, there will be fewer and fewer cases like this in the future.

My life is very different than I had imagined it would be. When I was fifteen years old, I remember making a class project on, "Where I saw myself in twenty years?" I said that I was going to be a pediatrician and have a wife with two to three children. I found that science was my worst subject when I was in college. I also thought I would be a teacher who could be straight. Eight years ago, I thought I could make myself fall in love with a girl who I knew from college who became a doctor. All along, the thread that ran through my life has been finding someone to love and share my life with. I have finally found that.

I am married now. I met my husband, Elliott, on March 26, 2015. Part of me wishes that I had met my him many years earlier to avoid my past mistakes. I didn't always choose the best for myself.

I thought our country was headed toward a brighter future for the LGBTQ, but the results of the recent presidential election have shown me how backward this country remains. I've never had to fully fight for my rights. My husband has been there for me to cry on and vent to as I respond to the persecution.

To those who are gay and waiting to come out… do it when you are ready. Don't let anyone else do it for you or tell you when you need to do it. I don't think I would have changed waiting until I was twenty-four to come out. That was best for me. It is your life and your story. Don't be ashamed if you're young and think you are in love with a member of the same sex. Love is a gift. If you happen to be in high school and have found someone of the same sex that you seem to have deeper feelings for, you may not want to miss out on the opportunity to let them know. Appreciate the support that people give but don't let anyone tell you how to live your life. There will always be people against you because they don't understand you, but there will always be more loving and compassionate people in your corner. Those are the types of people that you want to surround yourself with!

I have worked extremely hard to get to where I am today. I have found that it is important to never give up. The pain has made me stronger. Have hope. People have fought for your rights so don't be afraid to claim them. Reach out to those who may have different viewpoints than your own. Your life might just be the catalyst that changes hearts about the gay community.

Always remember that you bring something valuable to this world that no one else can bring…you.

*Luca moved to a more affirming city in the southern part of the country with his husband. He is a speech-language pathologist and works with children. He hopes to offer this service to a broader audience through his own business one day.*

# Thomas

## Chapter 13

*When Thomas came out to his family at age twenty-five, they were shocked. He did not fit what they believed was the gay "profile." His mother always told him that he was "easy to raise." He was kind and compassionate. He found learning enjoyable and became an exceptional student. He won several awards for excellence in sports and music activities. Whenever he committed himself to something, Thomas excelled in it. Having same-sex attraction was the one thing in his life that, as hard as he tried, he was unable to conquer.*

### Thomas's Story

I first became aware of being attracted to the same sex when I was in grade school. We received yearbooks each year and I would examine the pages to find the "cutest boy" and write those words on the photo. I also searched for the "prettiest girl," but the boys interested me much more.

When I moved on to middle school, I developed crushes on several boys in my classes and in my neighborhood, but I never told anyone.

By high school, I was fully aware of my feelings for the same sex. It was torturous to have feelings for others and be unable to express them. I did have many friends, however, both male and female. But, I knew no one who was gay, so I kept my identity quiet and I never told a soul.

I grew up in a mid-western town with my mother and grandmother. My mother was only eighteen years old when she had me. She and my dad were together for only a brief time and had divorced by the time I was three, so I have no memories of our being together as a family. I had periodic visits with my dad until I was an adolescent and then the visits stopped. I haven't seen him since. So, I grew up very close to both my mom and my grandmother.

We also had a large extended family nearby, so I had the advantage of growing up with them. My aunts and uncles were always supportive of my mom, which gave us a very fulfilling life. Some of my fondest memories involve my extended family. I remember gathering at my great-grandmother's house for holidays: grandparents, aunts, uncles, and cousins all there to celebrate together. I was an only child, so being with a large family made my life feel complete.

When I was six, my mom moved to Florida to find suitable work to support us, while I stayed with my grandmother. My grandmother and I joined my mom in Florida when I was eight.

While in Florida, I was exposed to much more diversity than in the mid-west, which contributed to my heart for justice and developed in me a sense of compassion. So, when we moved back to the mid-west before I started high school, though I was thrilled to be near my cousins again, it was challenging to live in an all-white community. My high school was extremely racist. A few racist students were part of the large group I hung out with, and I found myself speaking out against racism often. That was how I met Leslie, who would become one of my closest friends; she also had a heart for justice, and we grew very close.

In the light of the high amount of racism I observed at school, I knew not to bring up my sexuality. I felt comfortable with my friends because my sexuality was not in question as far as they were concerned. I kept my same-sex attractions inside in hopes that they would simply vanish from my life.

My mom had had a negative experience in her church while growing up, so she chose not to "force" me to practice any religion. She was a spiritual person, but she found her religious education to be filled with hypocrisy, guilt, and shame, and she wanted to protect me from that. We talked about it one day when I was in middle school. She said, "Believe what you believe." It felt a little strange for me to not have formal religious teaching while my friends were going through Sunday school, confirmation, and such. I just needed to figure it out for myself. I wondered about what I might be missing.

In a non-religious way, I tried to pray my same-sex attraction away. I journaled often and poured out all my emotions but as hard as I tried, I was unable to change.

About this same time, I started to look toward the future, and hopes and dreams took root in me. When I tried to imagine my adult life, I thought about what it would be like to have a husband. Could I do that? There was no information about the gay life at the time; no social media, Facebook, pro-gay television shows, or politicians fighting for gay marriage. I knew no one who could answer my questions. I was alone.

Fortunately, I was involved in many activities that kept me busy and socially active. I played soccer and ran track. I was proficient on the French horn, trumpet, and baritone and played in several bands—even traveling for music competitions at other schools. I also loved the outdoors, so I was involved in Boy Scouts.

High school was where I developed a love for psychology. Math and science were always my strong suits but when I took classes in psychology, something felt different. It all made sense to me, and I wanted to absorb as much as I possibly could. The courses expanded my mind and challenged me in a good way. They caused me to think through the racism I had witnessed in terms of human behavior tendencies and patterns.

After I graduated from high school and headed to college, I knew I wanted to major in psychology. I received a great deal of feedback about that—especially concerns about how I could make a living in that field. I figured I could double-major if I needed to. I also took some religion classes and read in the field of spiritual readings. This helped to fill the space that I thought needed filling.

My best friend, Leslie, went to the same university and we landed in the same dorm. We registered for a few of the same classes and spent most of our free time together. Everyone thought we were a couple.

One night, during my sophomore year, after a few drinks, I decided to disclose my secret to Leslie. I couldn't keep up the charade anymore. It was funny because many of my peers considered me something of a "ladies' man." I found out later that Leslie was afraid I was going to tell her I was in love with her. With the intent of lessening the blow, I told her I was bisexual. Even so, she was surprised. But, that quickly moved to her being excited for me. Slowly, I started telling my other friends, but I did not tell my family until much later.

After college, I moved to an east coast city to get a master's in psychology. There, I started living my life as a gay man. I had my first boyfriend; we dated for a while and then moved in together.

It so happened that one of my professors was a lesbian. She was a wonderful, encouraging instructor who taught five of my grad school classes and became an influential mentor for me, not only academically but was encouraging as I began to explore my sexuality socially.

During grad school, I didn't see my family or call them very often. I was living a different life they were completely unaware of and I found it painful to keep the truth from them. I avoided them altogether.

Only when I was about to graduate with my masters, at age twenty-five, did I decide to tell my family. They were coming for graduation and would be meeting my boyfriend so they needed to know. I didn't want to tell my mom and grandmother over the phone, but it couldn't be avoided.

The first person I told was my grandmother because she was easy for me to talk to and I knew she would be supportive. Even so, I poured a glass of wine before making the call. As it turned out, she was just as I expected, very supportive. She was, however, very surprised, and her first response was, "Don't get AIDS."

The next night, I called my mom. She too was very surprised. She was not disappointed in me but concerned about what she believed it might mean for my life. Her first response was that she was "so disappointed…no grandchildren." She adjusted quickly to my life as she gained a greater understanding about what that would mean for me. We are closer today than ever before.

I found it interesting that they were so surprised. I know there must have been signs throughout my life that may have suggested my sexuality. My mom told me that when I was little, I loved to brush her hair and told her I wanted to be a hairdresser. Not that every hairdresser is gay, but at the time, many were. But, I was so relieved that two of the most important people in my life were now aware and that they still loved me.

On reflection, I wish I had come out sooner. If I had known how supportive my family would be, I would have told them earlier. They love me unconditionally. If I had it to do over, I probably still would not have come out to my high school friends…not after witnessing the racism among them. Or, maybe senior year, I would tell them as I went out the door!

There are a few things I have learned through the years—I can trust my family. Family is number one in my life. There was a period when I thought that because I was the first in my family to go to college, I was different from them and did not need them any longer. That was not true. I am healthier and stronger because of my family. They love me unconditionally, like no one else.

The second is that I do not need to be afraid to "reinvent the wheel." Some old beliefs can be good but it's healthy to evaluate them and sometimes do things differently. Do not be afraid to create change.

I am now in a serious relationship with a person I hope to marry one day. I am learning how to balance my professional life and my personal life, which can be a challenge. To fully learn how to do that will probably take a lifetime of paying attention to what is most important at any given moment.

*Thomas is a psychologist at a large university in the northeast and engages in clinical practice and research. He lives with his partner in the city, near the university.*

# *Jasper*

## Chapter 14

*It was not until Jasper started the process that led to a physical change that he felt more like the person that he imagined himself to be. He was born Catherine but began to feel uncomfortable in his own skin when he hit puberty. He is a twenty-nine-year-old transgender man.*

*A trans person can be gay, straight or bi. He considers himself to be bi-sexual because he is attracted to both sexes. But it is more than that. Jasper is not attracted to the gender itself but to the person, specifically, to the personality.*

### *Jasper's Story*

I was pretty clear about my preferences when I was a child. I had older stepbrothers and stepsisters, so I had no gender requirements set for me. I played with any toys that I wanted—My Little Ponies, ninja turtles, and matchbox cars. I loved *Star Wars* after receiving a VHS and a Jedi costume from my aunt, then made a lightsaber from an old broom handle that my grandmother found. She taught me how to sew so I made my own costumes from old curtains and scrap fabrics. I learned to read at a very early age. I remember making a Mongolian costume after reading a book about Mongolians and their horses. I did wear dresses. My mom told me that I would pick out the most heinous clothing with crinoline and such. I liked the clothing that reflected historical time periods…costumes. That interest developed into a love of history and reenactment later in life.

My parents were divorced before I was old enough to remember my dad living in the same home with us. They were two very different people and probably should never have gotten married. When they separated, we moved in with my maternal grandparents for a while. My mom was a vindictive person, so she used me as leverage against my dad. I did not see him as much as I would have liked. My dad was a musician who made his living driving a truck. He was always a really cool guy. My mom was a barmaid and a bar cook. She struggled with drug and alcohol addiction for a while. I did not have a very good relationship with her until I was much older.

My mom met my stepdad when I was eighteen months old and they started dating. When they moved in together, my stepdad's two youngest children moved in with us. He was quite a bit older than my mom, and his three children were much older than me. The youngest of his children was ten years older. They were very nice and would babysit for me often. They treated me like family. My mom and stepdad had my younger sister when I was two. Oddly enough, my dad and stepmother also had a baby a few days apart from my mom and stepdad.

I enjoyed a very large extended family growing up. I am very close to my grandparents, cousins, aunts, and uncles. My extended family often stepped in to care for my younger sister and me when life was difficult for my mom. They are an "in your business kind of family," in a good way. They included my sister and me in their family fun. We went on vacations together and to other outings. They may be a little crazy, but they loved us and looked after my sister and me.

Because of my mom's issues, I was raised partially in my mom's house and partially in my maternal and paternal grandmothers' houses until I was older.

My stepdad and I were very close. He was like my dad. When he and my mom separated, he continued to treat me like one of his own children. He was a wonderfully kind and loving man. I always felt very loved and cared for by him. He was a good listener and very easy to talk to but I never shared with him my deepest secret.

I started to feel different from other children when I was in late middle school and early high school. Puberty was an absolute nightmare for me. I remember when I started to menstruate, my mom thought it was a big deal. She let me stay home from school and took me out to lunch with her friends, talking constantly about how I "was a woman now" and was special because of it. Woman power!! The problem was that I did not feel special, nor did I identify with being a woman. As my breasts started to develop it became more and more difficult for me. It was horrible in fact. I hated everything about what was happening to my body. I heard, "This is what girls do," but I did not feel like one.

I often struggled with anxiety and depression throughout my life. Puberty caused them to skyrocket in me. I was a male in a female body, so I decided to talk to a therapist. After explaining my situation, the therapist said that I "just needed a makeover to make myself feel pretty." That was not helpful! The second therapist told me that I would "grow out of it." I "just needed to have more female friends." A large majority of my friends were guys. Her comments made me feel worse about myself. The message it conveyed was that what I was feeling was wrong.

I was always a good kid. I never skipped school or got into trouble. I had many interests in and out of school. My life revolved around horses, art, and history.

Money was tight when I was growing up so I did not start riding horses until I was in my teens. I often worked at the barn to pay for lessons. When I got my own horse much later, I worked at the stable to pay for board. Ninety percent of the work was mucking stalls. Much later, I worked as a stable manager. I no longer have my own horse but have many friends that generously allow me to ride theirs.

I also was involved in the art honor society and participated in art exhibitions while in school. I have always loved the arts. My love of history, historical costumes, and reenactment became an interest during this time and has continued to be a focus today. Writing was also a love of mine. I journaled often and even had a book of poems published when I was in middle school. It was a really big deal. I got to meet the mayor as a result. I also was involved in music and sang in the chorus.

I went to a very diverse, over-crowded high school. Many students were bussed from the city and there was a large international population. My circle of friends included both males and females; many of the males discovered they were gay, later.

In sophomore and junior year of high school, in my desire to fit in, I decided to try to be more like a girl. I even had a boyfriend. I wore hippie-type clothing and dressed goth and my hair was long and hung below my waist. My aunt thought she was helping me by buying clothes that were black and lacey, but I felt like I was wearing a costume—playing a character in my own life. I was going through the motions and I was miserable.

For a short time, I thought maybe that I was a lesbian, but I was largely attracted to guys. I had a boyfriend that said he was bisexual but when I told him I thought I was a lesbian he mocked me and turned it into a big joke. That ended the relationship.

At the time that I was examining my sexuality, the gay community was beginning to get a lot of visibility. Gay rights were in the forefront. This was great but there was still no conversation about those people who feel like they were born in the wrong body, the transgender population. LGBTQ were all grouped into the same category when they really are so very different.

I was seventeen years old and it was not until I made a connection with a math teacher at school that I really started to understand my identity. I needed algebra tutoring, and the math teacher took it upon herself to help me improve my grade. She was training to be a therapist and it did not take long for her to assess that I required counseling. After sharing with her what I had been experiencing, she talked to me about the LGBTQ community, focusing on transgender issues, suggesting some resources that might be helpful.

The Chase Brexton Medical Services was, and still is, an organization that provided compassionate care for people in the LGBTQ community. I met with a doctor that counseled the transgender community and shared my situation. We discussed possible options, which included hormone therapy. The doctor also connected me to a support group for transgender people and I began meeting with them weekly. The group was led by a transgender woman. As I sat and listened to the stories, I had an epiphany. This was what I was experiencing. This was me!! It was encouraging to know that I wasn't the only person on the planet going through this. There were other trans people out there.

Back at school, the same math teacher that was so supportive of me took on the position of leading the LGBTQ club. It was a very small diverse group, only about five people. This small LGBTQ community stood out and became a target for abuse. The group received much teasing and was pranked constantly. Our teacher tried to help put a stop to it. I found out later that she was a lesbian but was not out at school.

Because I did not know how my family would react to my situation, I did not tell them. We did have other gay people in our family, but no one really talked about it. One of my aunts is gay, as is one of my cousins. I found out later that my aunt left home at age seventeen because her parents did not approve of her sexual identity. No one in the family seems to have a problem with them now.

My relationship with my mom was never very good but it became increasingly violent when I was in high school. I had a car so I could escape when I needed to and stayed away from home as much as possible.

After I graduated from high school, I took what I thought was a grand step of liberation and cut off my long hair. It was quite liberating but it did not end well. It looked like a mess…kind of like a porcupine. A good friend came to the rescue with clippers in hand and shaped it up for me. Much better.

That summer, I went to England for two weeks with my boyfriend's family. When I returned, I packed up and moved out of my mom's home.

I was pressured to go to college after I graduated, so the next fall, I went to the University of New Orleans. Six months after I arrived, hurricane Katrina devastated the gulf coast. I worked there to help with recovery efforts for a while, then returned home to attend the community college. I loved to write so I majored in English and minored in medieval history.

Shortly after my return from New Orleans, I started hormone replacement therapy. This was the beginning of my change. I was twenty years old. It did not take long for my physical features to start to change. I did not see my family much during that time for fear they would respond to the transformation. When I did see them, I was sure to shave my face closely and wear baggy clothes that a butch lesbian might wear. They said nothing about the changes. I was living with my stepdad at the time. He never talked to me about the changes that were occurring in me but he did question my sister about the use of his razor. There I sat, my face was covered with razor burn and he commented to my sister that dull blades would give razor burn. I could see him looking at me through the corner of his eye. It was a caring message for me. I said nothing. I had been so afraid that it would change his feelings for me.

My stepdad died suddenly two years ago at age sixty-four from health issues related to smoking and drinking. I received a hysterical call from my younger sister and rushed to the hospital. The hospital staff had just resuscitated him before I arrived, and he was on life support. My mom was there to support my sister. When his heart stopped for the second time, my sister and mom left the room and I was the one to make the decision to let him go. I had the hospital staff remove the tubes from his body so my other siblings could remember him in a better way. We were all in shock. It was a terrible loss.

I remember trying to have a conversation with my aunt who was a lesbian because I thought she of all people would understand me. Her response was very unexpected. "Don't tell anyone." She was worried about how my grandparents would react. So, I told no one in my family.

When I told some of my friends, they were supportive of my decision. I did not lose any friends over it but I was terrified that my family would find out somehow.

Because I was so afraid of being shunned by my family, I prolonged the hormone replacement therapy to make it a gradual process for them. I was on HRT for nine years and my family still never said a word about the changes to my body.

I started to go by the name "Jasper" with my friends. I was born Catherine, but I never felt like a Catherine. Even in middle school, I chose to go by Cat because it did not sound so feminine. When my friends would mistakenly call me Jasper in front of my family, I would make the excuse that we had just been with our friend of the same name.

My sister revealed my "secret" one day to my mom. Apparently, she had been reading my journals for years, and was frustrated with me that day for some reason. She decided to hurt me in the only way she knew how. She told my mom that I was "trans" and was receiving treatment. My mom went ballistic. She immediately called me on the phone and started screaming about my decision. I could not figure out who would have told her. I had spoken to my two aunts, two years after starting HRT. They would never have told her. My mom let me know her source and continued to scream. She hung up the phone and called three additional times screaming and hanging up. My partner told me that it might be best for me to let the phone ring. My mom continued to call for one hour straight. After that day, she pretended that nothing ever happened.

On Christmas that year, my mom gifted me with a frilly peasant shirt, bell-bottoms, and jewelry. This continued for a few years. It was as if she was denying what was happening and it was extremely hurtful.

My anxiety grew to extreme levels. I began to have horrible social anxiety because I was constantly being "misgendered" when in public. This was very painful so I would not leave the house unless I absolutely had to. Even going out with my partner was difficult. This needed to change. I had grown weary of living life as two people, so I elected to have the surgery done to my top. Most trans guys bind their chests to look more like a man, but because I was asthmatic, binding would trigger a severe asthma attack in me. My only option was surgery.

At age twenty-eight, I was preparing to have surgery and decided that I needed to tell my family and friends about the decision that I had made. They were not surprised and treated me the same. My friends were very supportive. Many had suspected I was in the process of changing.

I found an excellent surgeon and planned to have the surgery soon after I told everyone, but the insurance company backed out on their coverage. Originally, the insurance company had told me they would cover the medical costs. After all the preliminary procedures were done, they told me that they would no longer cover that type of surgery. My legal counsel is still working out the details with the insurance company. So, I saved up the money, $7,000, and had the surgery done a year later. It was quite a very long year.

Having the surgery changed my life. I am no longer misgendered when I go out in public. People finally see me the way that I have always seen myself. And it is nice.

The legal system does make it difficult for transgender people. Not only do you have to change your name, but you change your gender marker. I am still in the process of changing mine. So, I am Catherine on my identification. It takes a great deal of time and effort to convince people that I am the same person on my identification.

I think that my experience of being transgender has been mild compared to that of most people. I have experienced some discrimination when I go out with my male partner. It is usually hearing snide remarks about my being gay.

Discrimination is really a big problem for many transgender people. The female→ male seems to receive less attention than the male→ female. Transgender females are seriously at risk for violence. They often get jumped and beaten up. It can be very scary being trans. I have a trans friend who was almost killed at a bus stop just because she was wearing a dress.

All types of discrimination have gotten worse since the new presidential administration was put into place. People inclined to bigotry feel emboldened to respond negatively to the LGBTQ community now. This increased harassment is worrying. Violence toward this community is on the rise. It's been horrible.

The controversy about bathroom use by the transgender community has been in the forefront as of late. It is frightening to have to use a bathroom in public as a trans person and I avoid it as much as possible. I myself have not been bothered in the bathroom but know people that have. Some have been physically removed from the bathrooms. Women are just as much of a threat to the trans community as men. This harassment has caused trans people to be constantly looking around, for fear of their safety

The bigotry that I have experienced most has been in the church. My dad's family was religious, especially my grandmother. They would take me to church with them on Sunday when I was young. I read the Bible and went to Sunday school. I can clearly remember that those who were supposed to be religious at church were not the most accepting toward people who were different. At age eleven, I recall hearing the priest pray for some parents in the congregation whose son was gay. I also have friends whose parents sent them to "pray away the gay" camp. As I got older, I witnessed religious groups protesting gay marriage. This did not reflect the love I believed the church was supposed to reflect. I am not even certain about God's existence now.

I have always thought that if you are a Christian that you should love everyone, but that has not been my experience. It appears that trans people "wig out" the church so I do not feel comfortable there. The comment that trans people are "going to hell" I have found to be judgmental and unkind, so religion is not a factor in my life. The response I have witnessed from the church has made me feel that I would be happier not being religious. The rules and the bigotry are highly offensive. I believe that if you are kind to people, you have achieved a good life.

We only have one life to live on this earth. My decision to become a trans man was a personal response to how I felt in my own body. I regret that I did not take the opportunity to do what made me happy sooner. I worried so much about what others would think of me. There are many resources on the internet now that were not available years ago. If you have questions about your identity go and talk to someone. Chase Brexton's excellent counseling and resources were very helpful to me. They have specialists in this field. You do not have to do this alone.

*Jasper is currently pursuing his degree in veterinary technology, specializing in large and exotic animals. He spends his time doing historical reenactment, medieval fighting and archery, building and playing medieval instruments, gardening, collecting orchids, geckos, and carnivorous plants, making jewelry, writing, fiber arts, horseback riding, cooking, German longshore fencing, building terrariums, has several species of poison dart frogs, and traveling. He remains very close to his step-siblings and continues to see them for celebrations and holidays. Jasper lives with his best friend from high school and partner of nine years in the northeast.*

# *Charley*

## Chapter 15

*Charley grew up in the south, living what most would see as the "American dream." Her parents have been married for twenty-six years. She has a brother who is two years younger. They had two dogs and two cats, in a large house with a small yard surrounded by a white picket fence...a perfect life. But from an early age, Charley discovered that her interests were inconsistent with what the gender roles of our society dictated. She was different from the other girls.*

### *Charley's Story*

My dad has been a most influential and important role model in my life. Wearing many "hats" throughout the years, he has been my coach, my high school principal, my math tutor, a man of God, and a loving and devoted father. My first season of organized soccer at age four, he was my coach. In fact, I have competed on very few soccer teams where my dad was not the coach. For as long as I can remember, he has challenged me to be a team leader, a fearless competitor, and most importantly, an individual that leads with integrity and authenticity. I was raised with the mentality to always give 110% to everything I do, because hard work will always pay off in the end. When I was playing sports, there was unlimited potential on the field. As a female, that is empowering.

My mom and I have butted heads, because of opposing views, for as long as I can remember. I have a vivid memory of being around five years old when my nature was revealed. I was with my mom in our old Toyota van complaining from the back seat, "Mom, I don't want to wear these boots! I don't like them!" I am not quite sure if they were uncomfortable, ugly, or what, but this was obviously the first sign of my stubborn and rebellious nature. Honestly, I think my boots were probably too feminine. This type of relationship with my mom continued for years.

Even at that young age, I wanted to be like a boy. I dressed like and had mannerisms that were more consistent with a boy. I would never wear skirts or dresses. I can recall being scolded often for burping loudly, not wearing a shirt, and for the number of jeans I ruined with grass stains. My mother, aunts, and grandmother frequently told me that I needed to be more "lady-like." My stubbornness would only allow me to do the extreme opposite. While I see some of my actions at this age in my life typical of any other rebellious youth, I now see that it was more about defying normalcy and expressing myself the way I wanted. I always had this aura about me that I did not give a damn about what other girls thought of me for hanging out with the boys.

Throughout life, my brother and I have experienced different stages in our relationship. As young children we often bickered and fought, mostly while playing sports, when our true competitive nature would emerge. I think we both had a competitive spirit, a winning mentality, growing up with our dad as the football coach. It was deeply rooted in our lives. My brother, often a sore loser, would pout and cry if he did not win and this would frustrate me. I was always "one of the boys" and feel confident in saying 90% of our fights stemmed from some type of sport, game, or competition.

I was raised in the church and was baptized shortly after birth. We were completely committed to the church, attending services on Sunday, vacation Bible school youth choir, Sunday school, etc., if these activities didn't conflict with a sports camp, of course. My brother and I frequently played kickball in the church yard and I was always picked early, just like one of the boys. This was when I first started noticing I was different. I constantly wanted to compete against boys to prove my "worth" as a female. I fit in with the boys my age, and with another one of my female best friends who was heavily involved in sports with me. We were inseparable. Caroline always made me feel like it was okay to not be "too girly."

I was in second grade when I began to experience attraction to girls. She was a friend's sister. I was intrigued and attracted to her femininity. I was young and did not understand it so I did not talk about it to anyone.

Much of my life revolved around sports and a wide range of recreational activities. I always wanted to spend the majority of my time outdoors. My parents would practically have to drag my brother and me back inside after sunset.

The happiest times of my life as a child revolved around the community and friendships I developed through playing soccer. Since my dad was my coach most years, I got to spend a lot of time with him. I really treasure those moments with him.

Most of middle school was challenging for me. While I struggled to understand my identity, I was also attempting to fit in and be "popular." Sports really assisted in brightening up this stage in my life, particularly with my close friends and teammates on the basketball team and junior varsity high school soccer teams.

It really became clear to me how different I was from the other girls at a state-wide student conference on creating a space for global awareness. The conference focused on issues and creating legislature that would resolve individual countries' primary issues. Most of my friends at this age were beginning to obsess over makeup and how they looked for guys. One of them was my closest friend. She pleaded with me to allow her to put makeup on me for the dance that night at the conference. Me being the follower I was at that age, finally gave in. I have been fighting gender norms ever since.

It was also in middle school that I had my first real feelings for a girl. I was in seventh grade. I tried to suppress my feelings and prevent others from knowing about me by dating boys for a few weeks, here and there. I felt no real attraction to them, but I could disguise my inner life that way.

In high school, I continued to pour myself into sports. Once again, my happiest memories involved my teammates in soccer, basketball, track, and tennis. Unfortunately, not everyone appreciated my giftedness in sports. Off the field, people began to recognize that I was different from the other girls and unkindly drew attention to me. It really angered me when a male classmate constantly called me "Charles," the masculine version of "Charley." It did not help that I was never satisfied with my self-image, feeling extremely uncomfortable in feminine clothing. Most of the time, I would just wear athletic attire to school so I was comfortable. Again, I was defying gender norms.

Medical issues made life even more complicated in high school. Along with the fun of sports came multiple concussions, which needed to be addressed. I was also on a strong medication to control acne. Research has since proven this medication causes extreme mental and emotional stress, along with other issues. I experienced a lot of anger and emotional imbalance in my later years of high school, which I believe was a side effect. This dramatically affected my experience in school.

In my attempt to live a "normal" teenage life, I remained in a verbally abusive relationship with a boy for several years. I was trying to be "straight" and had not made the connection between my unhappiness and my sexuality at that point in my life. His family was having some problems so it was easy to stay around to lend support. I cared about them so there was an emotional attachment. My compassionate heart and people-driven personality would not let me end the relationship until much later.

When I went away to college, I noticed a dramatic change in my relationship with my brother. We had been so close. The first couple years, my ego blamed it on his girlfriend and what I perceived to be her negative influence on him. Any time I was visiting home from college she was around, and we were never able to spend quality time together. As I reflect on my life, I now realize how very unhappy and negative I was during my last two years of high school and first year or so of college. I believe that this played a major part in disconnecting from him.

I discovered that though my brother and I are very different in most respects, our basic values are very similar. With my brother being a staunch republican, and I, strong in my liberal views, we each saw the world through a different lens. This perception has since changed. After playing division I football as the punter his first two years of college, he realized that football was not for him so he joined a fraternity. He was quickly promoted to vice president soon after and transitioned into the role of president. He took his position very seriously and his response to an incident that happened really caused him to earn my admiration. My dad shared the story with me. One of my brother's fraternity brothers had been arrested for an act of domestic violence. On hearing this, my brother took the initiative to remove the guy from the fraternity house. While we may not agree on many things, we were raised with strong morals. We were raised to treat everyone with a mutual respect and to know that violence is never the answer. I have genuinely never been so proud of him.

My brother and I have not talked with each other about our personal lives for over six years now. I miss that. While this deeply saddens me at times, my hope is that one day we can overcome our differences and rebuild our relationship.

There were many times early in college when my interactions with women confirmed my sexuality, but I continued to deny it. My sophomore year of college, I worked with a girl who was out. We were very attracted to each other. We even kissed once but it did not continue because I was determined to deny my true identity.

As time went on, just as I began to realize that denying my sexuality was more difficult than I thought it would be, I was outed unwillingly via an anonymous non-affiliated Twitter account. I remember being at a fraternity party and someone saying "Charley is a lesbian? Well damn, we already knew." I remember feeling angered and embarrassed at first. Some of my closest friends were with me when we saw that tweet. They laughed it off and made me feel less uncomfortable. Later, I found out that they already knew and were just supporting me until I felt comfortable enough to tell them. A short time after, I decided to own it and walked a bit taller with a little more pep in my step from that day forward, but I had still not admitted it.

I was twenty-one when I began to share my authentic self with others. My last semester of college I finally told one of my best friends, Kenzie, who I'd met through working in the campus recreation center. I had developed a close friendship with her about two years prior. She was insanely supportive and encouraged me to be myself. Later, I found out that she was waiting for me to come out, as were many others. I remember feeling this overwhelming sense of relief. I had finally shared my "darkest" secret with someone close to me, who I trusted above anyone else. Kenzie continues to be one of my closest friends. Her compassion, kindness, and generosity genuinely touch the lives of many. I continue to share my deepest thoughts and most embarrassing moments with her, even though we are two thousand miles apart now.

It was in college that I began to experience persecution from the church. Some Bible thumpers tried to challenge the fact that God was my Lord and Savior...because I was gay. This past winter, an old teammates' father, a Southern Baptist, commented on a Facebook post telling me, "You will have to face God for your sins and you are going to Hell." Those words stung. I strongly believe that God made me the way I am, and He loves me to no end.

It was the summer of 2013, while living in the northwest for an internship, that I could finally fully accept and value my sexuality. When I returned home after the internship, to the southeast, I kept this to myself for the first six months. I had a dear friend from work that was gay and would frequently hang out with her and her partner. I identified with them and longed to be as comfortable about my sexuality as they were.

One by one, I began coming out to my family. The first family member that I came out to was my cousin Diane. I was going to a conference on campus recreation near her home. She lives in California and is in the same career field as me. She is not just a family member but a mentor, colleague, and friend. She introduced me to a career path that I have fallen in love with. Her passion for student development is contagious, and she continues to challenge me to be better personally and professionally daily. Her response was very encouraging.

In January 2015, I came out to my brother. I was traveling for work, was near his college and invited him to lunch. My brother is a very laid-back guy. After telling him my story, he responded with, "Okay." Then he told me that he loves me the same as ever. He was great.

I delayed coming out to my parents for about three to four more months. It was June 2015. I would go home on a weekend with every intention to tell them but did not. I had an elaborate plan in place. I thought of every conceivable question they might ask, with a pre-meditated response. Every weekend seemed to not be "the best" because I didn't want to ruin my parents' weekend; Easter and Mother's Day came and went.

I finally worked up the courage shortly after I entered a relationship with my first girlfriend. That made it quite a bit easier. I was probably more nervous to tell my parents than almost anything I have experienced in life. I remembered thinking while in college that I wanted to wait until I finished my undergraduate degree. I had heard horror stories from people about how their parents had completely cut them off financially when they came out to them and I was pretty reliant on my parents for financial support at that time in my life. Finally, I worked up the courage right before they went to bed one night. I became extremely teary-eyed when I told my mom. I started with "I have something I want to tell you." How I worded that is still a blur to me today, but I remember my mom's response was to play "20 Questions" with me. "How do you know? When did you find out? Is Zoe your girlfriend?" After 20 Questions and lots of tears, they told me they would love me and support me regardless of my sexuality. To this day, I can still remember my dad's look of compassion and his soft smile. His eyes told me he had somehow known for some time. This was so reassuring. My parents have been mostly supportive of me. My mom made a comment about my wearing men's ties, saying that my dad does not like it when I wear them. It was hurtful. She is coming around. Over the last six months she has been liking my posts on Facebook, which she never did before.

It is surprising how many people have shared with me about their sexuality since I have come out. Many family members identify with being queer; two great uncles, a great aunt, and a couple of cousins. My closest friends that I worked with in the campus recreation center were queer. One of them I shared a deep physical and emotional attraction to, but it was far too early in my development and understanding of my sexuality to express it. Another friend, I am still close with today. She and her partner have been with me throughout my journey from when I was a close-minded, privileged female in the closet to an open-minded and free-thinking queer feminist. I admire them for challenging the way I think and view the world, its people, my sexuality, and my femininity.

I think the community I grew up in and socioeconomic status played a critical part in my coming out story. Our small southern town, in a middle-class environment, looked at being gay as being abnormal. So, I stayed in the closet for a long time.

I have discovered, over the years, that my home church family is not as open as I believed them to be. Over Christmas break one year, a sermon was given by the high school basketball coach about how homosexuality is a sin. Six people from the team came out after they graduated. Once I became publicly out about my sexuality much later, and because of the way that I dress, I have been treated differently by many individuals from the church where I grew up. People are not as friendly anymore. I do not feel welcome there. So, I am pursuing an individual walk of faith and I listen to sermons online.

The discrimination I have experienced has been infrequent but painful. Fortunately, early on, I did not face much discrimination other than the occasional "dyke" comment from an enraged intramural participant. This past winter, however, I was attending a campus recreation conference that was held in a hotel convention center at the same time a conservative political conference was being held. Our association is heavily diverse and supports equity and inclusion to the extreme. You can imagine the intermixing of those people did not go over well. Very well-known politicians attended their conference to speak. This was the far right at its finest. I usually dress outside the gender norm, rather masculine, and when at a conference, am always dressed in a suit and tie. The number of nasty looks, mutters, and comments I received those few days were uncountable. I have never felt so unsafe in my life, and that's coming from someone who is from a small southern town.

My spirituality has really expanded over the past few years, after traveling through many countries and moving to the pacific northwest. I have opened my mind to being connected to God in new ways. God does remain my Lord and Savior. I try to practice love and compassion daily. However, I believe the criticism I have received from Bible-thumping Christians because of my sexuality has created a heavy divide between myself and the church. So, I seek God in other ways.

My hope for the future is that as stories from the LGBTQ community are shared, a respectful dialogue will result, causing a shift in the way the far-right views social equity on many levels, particularly regarding homosexuality.

If you had asked me how I imagined my future life to be around puberty, it would have been much different than it is now. I would have predicted that I would be married with kids and working as a teacher in my hometown. What a total 180 degrees! Upon reflection, I genuinely feel that gender norms, specifically the relationship with the church and its disapproval of homosexuality, really played a role in my concept of the "American dream."

I'm 24-years-old now and living in the northwest. In 2013, I found where my passion meets my purpose—pursuing a career in campus recreation. My life is now a place that I can thrive. I am expressing my true self—a lesbian feminist. Being a social justice advocate and educator of college students is a primary focus. I try to live a life of compassion, gratitude, and deep love and appreciation for people of all walks of life and faith.

My experience has taught me some life-changing lessons. Remember that those that love you will support you and continue to love you, regardless of their religious beliefs. Those that do not support you are not worth your energy or anxiety. Go slowly. It is a delicate process. Tell those you trust first—those who can be your allies and help you through the process. I wish I had been more confident when I first returned from the northwest instead of trying to suppress and hide it for a few months longer. I was heavily supported in my coming out process.

It is important to follow your heart. Be yourself…unapologetically. Stay true to your values. Do not let criticism discourage you. Live life with no expectations. When you take away expectations, you take away the necessity to live out the life others have dictated for you. It is unnerving and constantly consuming energy when you try to live someone else's life. Live the life you are created to live. You have been prepared for that. Once you start to live without expectations, you are lighter; you are freer. You have peace and are deeply happy. Find where your passion and purpose meet and thrive, every waking moment. Let your words bring healing, love, encouragement, and inspiration to others. You will never regret choosing kindness. No matter what, never stop chasing your dreams.

*Charley is currently working in the field of collegiate recreation as a recreation coordinator, overseeing intramural and club sports at a university in the northwest. Charley is professionally focused on globalizing campus recreation that enhances well-being internationally. She lives with her loyal companion, a beautiful black lab…who she says keeps her young.*

# Reckless

## Chapter 16

*Reckless has not been back to her hometown since she came out in November of 2016 because she fears what might happen. She grew up in the heart of Appalachia in a very backward, homophobic town where she witnessed persecution toward the LGBTQ community. She has chosen to avoid that by never going home.*

### Reckless' Story

My life has been a constant battle, beginning with my parents' divorce. I was a little over the age of four when my father left my mother. My dad is a veterinarian and owns his own clinic but never provided child support for my older brother and me. My mother worked three jobs to support us while my dad lived in a nice home with a pool and SUVs. At my father's home, I was upper middle class and lived that lifestyle. At my mother's, I was in the "working poor" class but, somehow, I never wanted for anything.

My father remarried my stepmother right away. My stepmother had been working at my father's clinic, which is how they met. It was shortly after when my half-brothers were born and life became even more hectic. Both of my parents wanted custody, so the court set a very dysfunctional visitation schedule that required my brother and me to see both parents every day, starting in kindergarten and ending when I was a freshman in high school. Each parent was also allotted one week's worth of vacation time with us over the summer. My father had gained a new life and a new family, and my stepmother was frequently angered that she and her family, my father and half-brothers, had to plan their lives around my older brother and me. Instead of feeling loved, I felt like an object being passed back and forth. It was exhausting, and it seemed like there was never enough time to simply be a kid.

My brother and I had an odd relationship. Early on, we were very close and he was everything that I wanted and needed in a big brother. However, as we grew older he became envious of me. He was three years older and somewhat introverted, while I was an extrovert and very sociable. I often got away with things that he would not have gotten away with. Looking back now, I see that there was wrong done on both ends that resulted in creating the odd relationship. The worst part is that he resented me for being so involved with activities because I did not have to work like he did at age fifteen. Life was difficult for the both of us, but I think he believed it was easier for me.

My mom worked hard and truly loved her children. It was evident in the way that she advocated for us. I still remember days when my father would pry my arms off my mother's neck, when I was four and five years old and the court-ordered schedule was a new thing. My mother had not gone to college and had a hard time finding a high paying job, so she started working three low paying jobs so that she could continue to provide for us. My mother remarried after one or two years and I gained two stepsiblings.

My father had a lot to juggle between his business, his new family, and his old one. I did love my father but was frequently confused by the decisions that he made. To me, life before the divorce was perfect and I couldn't understand why he had initiated so much change and there were times that I was very angry at him for doing so. Although I was hurt that he had chosen another family over the one that he already had, I also remember nights where he would soothe me as I held one of his fingers until I fell asleep.

Things slowly deteriorated between the two of us and it was during freshman year that I stopped going to my dad's house. I had just gotten back from a week-long vacation with one of my friends. It was 3:00 pm on Sunday afternoon and my mother was scheduled to pick me up at 6:00 pm. My father and stepmother left to go to the store and I was responsible for watching my little brothers. When 6:00 pm rolled around, my father was still not home. My mother had arrived to pick me up and I could not leave my little brothers alone. I called my dad more than twenty times and my mother was getting impatient. After fifteen minutes or so my father came home and told me that I was not allowed to leave. My dad wanted the week that I had gone to the beach with a friend to be considered my mother's vacation week with me even though she had not gone. He wanted an additional vacation week with me at his house. When I refused, he became very angry and said that I was out of control and a bad child. The last thing that he said to me was, "If you leave with your mother instead of staying here for a week, don't come back." So, I didn't.

After nearly a year of not speaking to my father, Christmas time rolled around and my older brother, who was still going back and forth between both parents, brought me a Christmas present from my stepmother. I was confused that she sent me a present but opened it anyway. The inside contained a ring box and a bag, so I opened the ring box first. Surprisingly, something other than a ring was inside. The ring box was filled with dog feces and the bag was filled with rotten lettuce that had become liquid. There were many times following that experience that my father wrote me letters telling me how horrible I was and that my mother had corrupted me. I grew to despise my stepmother and was extremely hurt by my father.

Before the split from my dad, between sports and seeing both parents daily, I was a very busy girl. I was an athlete and did cheerleading from first grade through my junior year of college. Gymnastics accompanied cheerleading, so I had some sort of practice almost every day during the week and some competitions on the weekend. I played soccer from seventh grade through senior year of high school and turned down a full scholarship to play collegiate soccer. There was not much room for anything else.

I found it much easier to talk to women growing up so they became my closest relationships. In fourth and fifth grade, I had several infatuations with female role models in my life. At that time, I thought that my obsession with women was just a need for attention. I remember experiencing same-sex attraction as early as third grade. I had no real interest in dating boys but fell into peer pressure and the preconceived idea that I was supposed to be with them.

As early as fourth grade I dated boys because I assumed that I was supposed to be straight. I did not allow myself to even explore the thought of being a lesbian. Every church that I had ever been to spoke against it and Christianity was very important to me. The churches in my hometown used the slogan "turn or burn" and being gay was said to be an unforgivable sin that would send you into an eternal fire pit. It was unsafe to be gay.

I only knew of two gay men in the entire town and only one of them was open about his sexual orientation. One of the guys was one of my closest friends in middle school and he refused to go to the county high school because he feared that he would be harmed by those who were homophobic. Back then, he said that he didn't want to attend the county high school because the city school had better academics, but we knew of high schoolers at the county school who had already been mean to him for being feminine. It was a rough awakening for my group of friends. I had gone to school with him since preschool. Knowing that he wouldn't attend the same high school instilled a deeper fear of what being gay might do for my safety and I cowered even deeper in the closet.

In high school, I tried to make myself attracted to guys and dated them during my freshman year and half of sophomore year. I loved making friends and got along with pretty much everyone. It was confusing for me dating guys and pretending to be straight. Each relationship that I was in with a boy felt forced and uncomfortable. It was like I had to invent ways to be "in relationship" with them because it felt so wrong. After several failed relationships, I thought that I had just not been with the right guy and even convinced myself that if I had sex with a guy, I would somehow start liking men. That experience woke me up to the reality of my identity. I never had sex again but I continued to attempt dating guys. By the end of sophomore year, I thought "maybe I am not meant to date anyone." So, I did not date anyone from sophomore year to senior year. I threw all my time into soccer and cheerleading and being the very best friend to others that I could be. Being a good friend was important to me and somewhat filled my need for relationship with others.

Before my freshman year in high school, I went to church with my dad. After our falling out, I did not go to church until junior year. Growing up in a non-denominational church that was highly influenced by surrounding Pentecostal and Baptist churches was somewhat good for me in terms of creating community with others. I was saved at the age of seven and thought I knew what Christianity was all about. I was close with the youth group, and my group of friends often got together outside of church. I thoroughly enjoyed church until I was in middle school, because it was around that time that I started having disputes with my father and stepmother and did not enjoy being around them. There was a time that I was sick on a Sunday morning and did not get out of bed to get dressed for church and my stepmother forced me to go anyway. I was wearing my pajamas and I was not allowed to change clothes. During the service, my stepmother approached the pastor and asked him to pray for me because I was becoming rebellious and an "evil" child. The pastor prayed for me and "laid hands on me" with several others. This event tainted the way that I viewed the church and no longer felt welcome in any church setting.

During the summer between sophomore and junior year, I went to a Christian conference and had a spiritual experience like no other there that prompted me to recommit my life to Christ. Carl Lentz, one of the speakers, told a story about the way he would tell his daughters positive attributes that they held so that when the world started trying to influence their identity, they would be able to confidently say, "My Father (God) says___" instead. I thought about my relationship with my father and thought that if I could be forgiven by God for all the bad that I had done, there was some way that I could forgive my father for what he had done.

Junior year, I started going to church with a friend and began to experience God differently than I had in the past.

I was thankful to be forgiven. I did a lot of bad things during my freshman and sophomore year in high school, most of which were the result of trying to convince myself that I liked men. For example, during freshman year I had dated an older guy, a freshman in college, and he took full advantage of my fragile state, taking inappropriate photos of me. Long story, short, the guy that I had been dating started dating a new girl and she found the photos on his computer. She became enraged and decided to send the photos to everyone on his email list, which included nearly all my teachers and friends. The ones that received the pictures via email forwarded them to more people and soon the entire high school had seen them. My older brother and mother found out about them and there was a period of roughly a year that they looked at me as if I was horrible. When I attended the Christian conference, most people had forgotten about my past. I, however, had not, which led me to find peace and comfort in knowing that God forgave me for the horrible things that I had done. God helped me to begin to forgive myself and others. After that year, I slowly began talking to my father again.

The college I attended the following fall had a culture that was much more open to the LGBTQ community. I majored in sociology. Sophomore year, I took a sociology class that was taught by a lesbian. She was married to a woman who also worked at the college. I saw the way they interacted with one another and it resonated with me. I wanted that in my life. At that moment, I realized that I was gay. It was difficult for me to accept this fact, due to my Christian beliefs. I remember praying multiple times during the day asking God to take the burden away from me.

In the middle of my sophomore year, I met someone through mutual friends. She was a lesbian and pursued me. I was extremely vulnerable; I had not told anyone about my sexual orientation and therefore had no one to discuss it with, and immediately responded. We talked for a while then started dating. I really didn't like her emotionally, physically, or spiritually but it was comforting to have someone to talk to about being gay and the reality of it. We ended up dating for two years and no one knew about us. She went to another college. so it was easy to lie about where I was going and what I was doing. I was popular and lived in a sorority house, so people were constantly asking me where I was going so frequently. Lying became an everyday thing for me to do. The relationship was not good, although I convinced myself that it was for almost a year and a half. The woman was very manipulative and required that I see her every two weeks. My life became an intense schedule of friends—home—girlfriend—classes. It was crazy. She also communicated with me constantly through texts. If I did not respond to her within a couple of minutes she became furious. She isolated me from all my friends and made it so that I was only close with her. She controlled every moment of my life. I was not allowed to go to fraternity parties or drink with my friends. I was not allowed to go to my sorority formals. She even became hostile toward me when I became a sociology tutor, simply because that meant I would be spending time with other people. She was extremely abusive and sexually assaulted me more than ten times. Further, she often did things to me that would cause me to have panic attacks and thought that doing so was funny. She would also come into the bathroom while I was showering and take pictures of me while showering, although I always locked the door, she would unlock it and barge in. She violated me frequently.

At the end of my junior year, I became more depressed than ever. I thought it was because I was not out yet, which was a lie that my girlfriend told me. I wasn't allowing myself to see the abuse that was happening to me and my girlfriend tried to divert my attention elsewhere.

At the beginning of my senior year, I started seeing a counselor. We tried to find the root of my depression and the counselor asked me to write down every time I was anxious. After doing this for a week, I realized that every anxious moment involved my girlfriend. As I came to the realization that I was being severely abused, I started ending our relationship slowly. First, I stopped talking to her so frequently by telling her that I had a group assignment that I needed to work on or that I had a paper due the next day. After doing that for several weeks, I told her that I needed some time to myself to think about things and after a month I broke things off between us. I told her that I was not going to do it anymore. She responded with the threat of "outing" me and threatened to send the nude photos of me that she had taken while I was showering to people that I knew.

You probably wonder why I endured such a difficult relationship. Why did I put up with it for so long? I had heard since childhood from the church and culture that no one would accept me because I was gay. I was heavily involved with my college's gender and women's society, and planned events like "Take Back the Night." I knew what abusive relationships looked like and people often came to me for advice on how to get out of them. It's different when it happens to you, though. I just wanted to be loved and accepted.

After escaping the traumatic relationship, a sorority sister who was an alumnus, started badgering me about what was going on. I innocently shared with her and thought nothing of it. Six months later, I noticed that my roommate started acting strange toward me. A week later, after returning to the dorm, my roommate locked the door behind me and confronted me. Apparently, my sorority sister had shared everything with many and it made its way to my roommate. I told my roommate the truth, that I was gay. The first thing that she said was, "You have been in this room with me. You have watched me change." I quickly reassured her that I had no romantic feelings toward any of my sorority sisters and that they are like my literal siblings. Then, she felt disappointed that I had been through so much trauma and did not share it with her. She was mostly sad that I had to endure such pain on my own. She became most accepting of me and we remain friends to this day.

The sexual assault and abuse left me with post-traumatic stress disorder. I would have night sweats and terrors and feared going to sleep. I slept very little...usually from 4:00 am to 8:30 am. I was triggered by almost everything around me. Seeing the same car that she used to drive, hearing certain words, even movies shown in class, caused me to have flashbacks of being raped. That winter, I began to fill my life with my friends and it brought health to my soul. Recovery from abuse is not linear… it's more closely related to a roller coaster. I had days that I would wake from night terrors paralyzed, unable to get out of bed. I had others where my friends would drag me out of my room to keep my mind off things. I was majoring in sociology and religion and decided to come out to my religion professor that winter. We were discussing my thesis, "A Feminist Theology of the Cross as Liberation." It was empowering for me to study the liberation model and learn about the strength we gain through the resurrection of Christ. But, after my horrible experience of abuse, I found it difficult to read some of the material as it related to minorities, particularly women, and the struggle to gain liberation from abusive relationships when using theology that included the classic atonement models. I started talking to the professor about changing topics and shared about my abusive relationship. She was awesome. She asked if family and friends knew and said that I would need that support. Regardless of what happened, she said that I was strong and would get through it and that the liberation model would be helpful for healing. She met with me often to discuss things and to make sure that I wasn't being triggered by the material and checked in on me often. After a lot of support from her and my counselor, I completed my thesis and my sociology and religion majors.

After sharing with the professor and with my counselor, I started attending their church. I went to the contemporary service. It was welcoming and affirming. I was reminded of God's love for me.

December 2015, I came out to my friends. My best friend was the first to hear the news. She knew I was something, gay or asexual, but was not sure which. Then

I came out to my other close friends. They knew that something that had been going on because I seemed different for the last two years, but they did not know I was having such a difficult time. They knew something was pulling me down. They were patiently waiting for me to share it. I remember them checking on me over winter breaks to see if I was okay. They were there for me even though they had no idea what kind of turmoil that I was experiencing. They cared for me and attempted to help me even when I did not know how to help myself. They were loving and very affirming.

Throughout my college career I attempted to make sense of my sexuality. I did a study during my senior year on the campus climate for LGBTQ+ students, primarily doing interviews with people involved in Campus Spectrum, my college's LGBTQ+ alliance. I had been involved in the Gay Straight Alliance since freshman year supporting those who were out. There were only five people that I knew of that were "out" on campus and I wanted to know why. Being gay myself and being somewhat in the closet caused me to evaluate the campus climate and want to see why others believed that LGBTQ people weren't out on campus. I interviewed people that were involved with Campus Spectrum and asked them questions about their understanding of the LGBTQ atmosphere on campus. I had been friends with them since freshman year, and I shared about myself because they were so open and honest with me. They kept my secret because they knew what it was like to be fearful of coming out. I also was vice president of the women and gender group. I found much overlap between those that were involved in Campus Spectrum and those within this women and gender group. Being around such open and affirming people allowed me to open up and feel confident in telling them who I was and who I wanted to love.

The July after graduation, I started talking to the woman who is now my fiancée, Boomie. We had been in the same sorority at the same college but were separated by five years. She was often an alumna for sorority rituals and events and we knew of one another through that. I had always had a crush on her and wanted to pursue her although I did not know if she was gay. I wasn't out and being in the abusive relationship caused me not to. After we started talking, I knew that we shared many of the same interests and values and that we would get along well. However, I was slow to allow myself to be in a relationship again. The last one had left me broken and I worried that I would not be able to date her without negative flashbacks occurring and messing it up between us. However, after much prayer and serious discussion with her, we began a relationship in August. At the time that we started dating, I was living with my older brother. He had gotten a job in the same town my college was located in, and I was interning at a local church for the following summer and fall. There were many nights when I stayed over at Boomie's and my brother would become very angry, saying that I was using his house as a storage unit. Although he was often angry at me for spending so much time away, he never knew exactly where I was staying, as I was still hiding my sexual orientation from my family. I loved being in Boomie's presence and wouldn't have done anything differently. I knew from early on that she was someone that I could see spending my life with.

In October, my mom called to ask if I was dating her. Since I had been living with my brother at the time, he must have shared. I felt no need to lie about it anymore and told my mother the truth. My mom explained that she was envisioning a different life for me and she cried, and cried, and cried. She did not say a lot during that conversation, but said that although she did not understand it, she wanted me to be happy.

In November of that same year, my dad's response was very different. "You are going to go to hell. You need to go to counseling. We did not raise you this way." A most unpleasant conversation via text message. He said that I had ruined his life and that he thought I was just being rebellious, once again. He would not talk to me face to face after that. One of my half-brothers offered his unsolicited opinion. "You have killed your father and ruined his life." Then, he continued to tell me how much my father's family hates me. I have not spoken to him since.

Although their reaction was horrible, it was not surprising. During my sophomore year, I tweeted that one of my favorite poets would be performing in a town nearby and that I wanted to go. The poet happens to be gay. My half-brother called a couple of minutes after that tweet to tell me that my dad and stepmother knew that I was gay and that they were both infuriated at me. He also said that they were cussing, yelling, and saying that I was demonic and that I had gone crazy.

When I became engaged, I decided that I would inform my dad before I let the world know on Facebook. I sent him a text but heard nothing for more than a day. When I called to see if he got the message, he replied, "I don't know who you are anymore. We didn't raise you this way."

"Can't you just be happy that I am happy?" I cried out.

Now he wants to get together to talk to me. He has hopes that he might "change my mind" and that I won't be gay anymore. I assured him otherwise, but he says that he wants to try to talk some sense into me. It's sad that my father, after all that we have been through, cannot accept me because of who I love. He treats me as if I have something seriously wrong with me—something that I could somehow spread to others. It is sad.

My mother continues to support me and all my endeavors and is very excited to help plan the wedding which will happen in July 2018. She has grown so much and has become more accepting of others by knowing that her own daughter is a part of the LGBTQ community. My father, however, will not discuss my sexual orientation or anything, and rarely communicates with me. Both my fiancée and I have tried reaching out to him, and the response is never different: there is no response at all. My older brother and I speak on occasion and he finds no fault in my being gay although we don't really get along generally. My half-brothers don't talk to me. I have tried reaching out and they do not respond. My stepmother pretends to be accepting of me, although past situations have made me weary of her.

Now I am employed by a human rights organization, working as an investigator of discrimination cases of race, age, and sexual orientation along with many other things. It is a perfect job for me because I am standing up for those who are persecuted. I used to think that being passive was better but, after studying the Bible and learning more about God and myself, I don't think Jesus Christ was ever passive. Jesus actively opposed violence with non-violence and through the power of truth, evil was exposed for what it is. This active, non-violent opposition challenged the people surrounding Him, and even us today, to recognize the great power that comes from compassion and through living up to our God-breathed selves. In the same way that Jesus confronted the systematic evil during his time through the power of non-violent interactions, so should humanity act upon our call to stand against oppressive forces and not let others take advantage of our kindness and love for humanity. I have grown closer to God than ever and am excited about the future that I have alongside Him.

In September 2017, I returned to seminary. I had taken a leave of absence because of the PTSD that put me behind on my collegiate career. I had to take an "incomplete" class during my final semester and finished my last class in August 2016. My GPA ended up being a 3.74, and I am quite proud to have gotten through the abuse with a decent GPA. I am really enjoying my studies now.

This crazy, difficult, amazing, joy-filled journey in life has taught me many things. The first, and the most important, is that people were created to live in community with other people. God is three persons and each of those persons are equally important as the other. We are called to be in relationships with the people around us…regardless. The great Leslie Knope once said that no one achieves anything alone, and I believe that to be true. People need one another to live fulfilled and whole lives. I have experienced firsthand that we flourish when we love and connect with others in the way that Jesus did.

The second lesson that I have learned is to volunteer as often as you can. The more that I give myself to helping the community around me, the more I start to find myself. By involving yourself in the liberation of those around you, you discover who you were meant to be as you treat others in the same way that Jesus does.

The third is to draw closer to God. It is a safe place where love resides. There have been many times that I have listened to certain church voices that tell me that I am not loved or accepted by God. I urge you to search further and to find the greatness and all-encompassing love of the Creator. There is no person that can outrun or outgrow the deep and broad love that God offers. I am challenged daily as I learn about new aspects of God. Advocate. Advocate. Advocate. Jesus works daily as our Advocate and it is our duty and privilege to advocate for all of God's creation. Take care of yourself, of others, and of the planet.

Having role models and advisors is very important. Look to them when making large life decisions for they can see things that you sometimes cannot. Allow close friends and those that you trust to give you advice. We sometimes find ourselves in situations where our judgment is clouded, and we need an outside party to help us see the correct point of view, especially when it comes to abuse. It is difficult to point out situations of abuse when we are in them and therefore we need others to share wisdom and love when we need it most.

Lastly, I have learned that it is okay to not be okay. Each of us have times where we carry burdens that cripple us. It is not God's intention for us to carry burdens alone, but for us to join alongside one another. A weight that might crush us if we carry it alone would become weightless if many people carry it together. Ask for help when you need it. Don't feel as if you will put too much pressure on others. There are people surrounding you that want to help relieve your burdens and would be happy to do so.

After all the things that have happened to me and all the things that I have done, I have truly found happiness. God is the ultimate source of our joy and He aches for each of us to live the life that He imagines. This life is one where we fully accept ourselves and love the unique craftsmanship of the Creator. Do not allow the world to convince you that God did not breathe life into your bones.

I have also found great joy in my fiancée, Boomie. She is a gift. I truly believe that we complement one another perfectly, and I am so lucky to have the privilege of loving her.

*"Reckless" continues to work as an investigator of discrimination cases. She will begin seminary in the fall*

*of 2017. She lives with her fiancée in the southeast where they are planning to wed.*

# *Todd*

## Chapter 17

*Todd had already started transitioning when he first met Katrina. They met on a dating site and chatted for two months before meeting in person. Todd really liked her, so he made the decision that he would not tell her he was a trans man until their third date. He really wanted her to get to know him first. So, he waited.*

*The timing of the third date couldn't have been more perfect because Katrina was scheduled to go on a business trip the next day. This would provide some space for her to think about whether she wanted to go forward with their relationship...or not. So, at the end of their third date, as Todd was walking her home, he told Katrina he was a trans man.*

### *Todd's Story*

As I reflect on my life, an overwhelming sense of gratitude wells up inside of me. My parents were pretty extraordinary; very loving and always very supportive. I was close to them both but in different ways. I loved the outdoors so my dad and I spent countless hours hunting and fishing. My mom was easy to talk to and offered advice when I needed it the most. Though my sister was three years younger, she and I had a special bond. We did not have the typical sister-sister relationship. We were more like sister and brother. Our interests really overlapped. We loved to play outdoors together and were on the same softball teams. But we were different in that my sister could also be very feminine…and I was not.

Our family was also very conservative and went to the Lutheran church every Sunday. When I was young, I really didn't hear anything from the church about the gay community, but I did from my family. I remember hearing early on that being gay was "abnormal." It wasn't presented in a hateful way, it was just matter of fact.

As early as I understood the difference between boys and girls, I knew I was different. At age four, I was often mistaken as a boy. My mom would kindly correct the person, but I could sense her embarrassment, so it began to embarrass me. I wore boys' clothes, shoes, and had mannerisms that suggested that I was a boy. I even tried to stand up when going to the bathroom. Everything about me said I was a boy and I often reminded my mom of that. In my mind, I was a boy.

At age five, when I was old enough to write, I began to express my feelings on paper. I gave myself a boy's name and once wrote, "My name is Danny. I am a boy. I have a penis." My mom was beside herself with worry. I remember her telling me, "I love you and would do anything I could for you but I can't make you a boy." She saved my writings and gave them to me when I was an adult.

I was a boy in a girl's body and it became increasingly frustrating for me. My mom's concern landed me in a therapist's office. She didn't take me there to change me, but to help me deal with my feelings. For two years, I went to the therapist to talk about how I was feeling, and I became more and more frustrated with the process. The sessions involved my talking about how I felt while I played with toys. I wasn't getting anything out of therapy, so I told my mom that I was "fine now" and did not need to continue. So, I stopped going.

I was constantly teased by the other kids because I was different. I was a girl looking and acting like a boy. I was called "gay," "boy-girl," and was asked why I walked so funny.

My interests helped to distract me from some of the social turmoil in my life, as did my best friend, Mike. He was faithful and accepted me and stood by me despite the teasing that I received. Mike came over to our house a lot. He was like my parents' third child. We loved everything about the outdoors and spent as much time playing in the woods as possible. My sister joined in with the fun until her friends came over. Their interests were so different from mine that we never played together.

I loved sports. Cal Ripken was my hero and I had my parents to take me to many baseball games early with the hope that I would get an autograph. That didn't happen until I took myself to a game in college. Success!

It was in elementary school that I started having crushes on the girls. I was so young that I really didn't understand it until I was older.

Middle school brought a whole new set of challenges as I remained a boy persona in a girl's body. I continued to be attracted to the girls but did not express it. Some of the girls didn't care if I was *different* but the teasing began to escalate from others. I was often asked if I had a penis.

Some kids were just plain hostile and combative wanting to fight with me. I got into a few "semi-fights," some pushing, shoving, and maybe one punch was thrown but no one ever got hurt.

Kids constantly harassed me and eventually started bothering my sister. One day, one of the major bullies threw rocks at her. When I told him to stop, he continued, so I jumped him and choked him. He broke free and ran home, never to harass my sister again.

After a while, Mike decided that the teasing became too much for him and he distanced himself from me. It was so disappointing but understandable.

It was in middle school that my interest began to broaden. I learned to ski and snowboard and this became a lifelong activity for me. I continued the softball that I had started playing when I was six years old, and added baseball, and biking, to my list of activities of fishing and hunting.

It was at this same time that I began to develop obsessive-compulsive disorder (OCD). I had always liked to organize and collect things when I was little, but as I got older I began spending more and more time organizing and straightening things in my room. It got to the point where I was spending much of my free time in my room making sure everything was where it needed to be. My mom became concerned and I found myself back in therapy. I was officially diagnosed with OCD, anxiety, and depression, and placed on medication.

There was nothing specific that triggered my OCD, it just began when I was young and progressively got worse as I aged. My mom and grandfather have both had to manage it in their lives, so it does run in my family. I have found medication helpful in controlling my symptoms through the years.

I continued to go to church and the youth group, but it was less than encouraging. We had moved to a non-denominational church and the anti-gay attitude there made me feel extremely uncomfortable. I knew I was different and it hurt. The kids who went to the youth group were the very same kids that made fun of me in school. This judgmental attitude made me decide to turn away from the church.

When I started high school, I decided to date a few guys so that people would stop talking about me being gay. I really wasn't interested at all and when guys would get too close, I ended it. I went to the junior and senior prom with guys for appearance's sake. One was a friend of a friend in a different school. There was a female couple that went to the prom together that caused quite a stir. I thought that was very courageous.

I was attracted to many of the girls but kept it quiet. I managed to remain friends with a group of girls from middle school through high school despite our differences. Talking about boys and going to the mall was not my thing so I opted out of that, but we spent many hours playing on the softball team together.

So, in high school, I busied myself with activities other than dating. I continued to love softball, baseball, fishing, hunting, and I learned to play the piano and the violin.

When I went to college, the trauma of dating in high school made it very difficult for me to consider putting myself in that position again, so I did not date in college. I poured myself into my studies, a double major in Business Information Systems and Accounting and worked part time in a department store freshman and sophomore year. Senior year, I took an internship at a retirement home in their IT department. This was a great opportunity and opened the door for a job after graduation.

Playing division III softball was a highlight of my college career. Unfortunately, because softball was a girls' sport, I have had to suppress discussing it with anyone that I have gotten to know post my transition.

In college, I became very attracted to one of my best friends but never acted on it. We played softball together and I knew that was going to have to be the extent of the relationship.

I remember telling two friends about the turmoil inside of me, my last year of school. We had played softball for years together so I believed them to be a safe place. I gave a limited explanation as to my situation. I told them that I was attracted to girls. I just couldn't complicate the issue with explaining how I felt uncomfortable in my own body. Their reactions were totally opposite. One of my friends was fine but the other reacted in such an abusive manner that I had to end our friendship. The one who supported me advised me to tell my parents right away. She was concerned about my fragile state.

The *coming out* experience with my friends was followed by a planned ski trip with a larger group of friends. I debated whether to go or not, but I loved skiing, had paid my part, so I decided to take the chance. It was just as I expected, extremely awkward with very little conversation and I just wanted to get through the weekend. So, I skied alone. Finally, it was time to depart and I discovered that a foot of snow had fallen the night before. Ugh! Carrying all my belongings, I trudged through the deep snow to the furthest side of parking lot and dropped everything behind my car. I was totally unprepared and had nothing with which to clean my car. Then God's love showed up in the form of a stranger to lend a helping hand. He said, "It looks like you need some help. Here I think you're going to need this," as he handed me a brush to clean off my car. We cleaned the car with little conversation, I thanked him and he was gone.

It was clear to me, at that moment, that God was letting me know that everything was going to be okay. I was going to be fine because He was looking out for me. God was revealing His love.

When I came out to my parents shortly after telling my friends, they responded as they usually did. They were extremely supportive and loving. Together, we immediately began researching for professionals that could help me manage what I was experiencing. It was then that we discovered the Hopkins Gender Clinic. The doctor was wonderful and instrumental in helping me to discover what I carried deep inside. This was the beginning of my transition.

After graduation, I took a job at the retirement home where I had interned while in college. I worked in the Information Technology department for two years, then put my accounting degree to work for the remaining five years in their accounting department. I tried very hard to live up to the expectations of others and looked more feminine than I ever had. My clothing and makeup went counter to all that I was feeling inside.

I attempted to date women but the fact that I was uncomfortable in my own body was not helpful. I just couldn't express my true self as a woman and the relationships I found myself in were unhealthy and abusive. So, I realized that I needed to do something about it.

My parents reacted pretty well to my dating women. My mom was very surprised but continued to support me. My dad actually surprised me. He expected that I would date women. Their love and selflessness has been a constant throughout my life. So, when I decided to transition to male they responded as they always have...with love.

In 2004, the transition commenced with six months of talking with a therapist about what might be the best treatment for me. I knew that living the way I had was no longer an option. There was so much to think about. Was a physical change the only way? I had to mentally prepare for whatever was to come. One of my greatest concerns was needles. This may sound humorous to some, but I really don't like needles and a physical change would require many. After six months of therapy, it had become clear that a physical change was the only solution.

There were so many things to resolve prior to the change. I needed to be completely ready for what was about to occur to my body. In preparation for that, I changed my name and had the necessary legal documentation completed. Hormone treatments began in 2005, six months after my decision. I was on hormone therapy for one and a half years.

I started to transition while working for the same company. The hormone treatments were working and I was looking more masculine. The therapist offered to come in to my office to explain to my colleagues what I was experiencing. I had told no one. I chose to go on a business trip to avoid the scheduled gathering. I did not want to be witness to the shock or uncomfortable questions or comments. It apparently was received very well. It did feel awkward for a while but that did pass. People were kind and gracious.

My body continued to transition. Then in 2007, I had top surgery. This was done locally by a specialist in the field. The surgery was a success and I began to feel more like the person I imagined myself to be.

Two years later, I decided to try dating again...as a man. I completed a profile on a dating site and began communicating with a lovely woman named Katrina. We connected online for two months before I asked her out. I wanted to see what kind of person she was and I wanted her to get to know me. Was she the kind of person that would be willing to enter in to a relationship if she knew I was a trans-man? So, I decided that I would not tell her until the third date.

We met at Starbucks for our first date. I thoughtfully bought her a chocolate chip muffin and a cup of coffee, only to find out months later that she really didn't care for chocolate. Still, she politely received my offering and we spent the next three hours getting to know one another.

The conversation just flowed. We had so much in common; similar backgrounds, values, and interests. At the end of the night, when the staff at Starbucks began to close the place, we said our goodbyes and I told her I "would be in-touch." Then, I called to see if she got home safely.

I had just moved into my new house prior to our date so with all the unpacking and settling in, the next date didn't happen for a while.

### Katrina's version

When I first met Todd, I thought, wow, what a handsome man. He is a little short, though taller than me. The last man I dated was six feet eight inches. I had a little anxiety about meeting guys because my last relationship didn't end well. That night, the anxiety quickly passed. Todd was different than my last relationship. He was easy to talk to and I found myself wondering if he was authentic. That was important to me. By the end of the evening, despite the chocolate chip muffin, I was convinced that I wanted to see him again.

Though he called to see if I got home safely that night, I was very disappointed that he didn't call me for a second date soon after that. I waited and waited for him to call, then I took control and asked him out.

### Back to Todd

Our second date was at the local Roy's. Once again, conversation was so easy. Katrina was cute and fun, and I really liked her personality. And most importantly, she was genuine. I was really starting to like her and began to experience anxiety about telling her the truth on our third date.

At the end of our third date, when we were close to her home, I told her the truth. I was direct. There really was no other way. So, I came out with, "I was not born male." Though she had some gay friends in college, Katrina had been very sheltered and knew very little about the LGBTQ community, especially transgender people.

She asked, "What does that mean?" So, I explained very clearly that I was born female and was transitioning to male.

### Katrina's response

Todd was the first person to ever utter the word "transgender" to me. I had friends who were gay and lesbian, but transgender was a whole new concept. I remember asking what it meant, thinking at first, that he physically had both forms of genitalia, not realizing he was born one way and had transitioned to look like he did that day. It was too much to wrap my head around.

Todd was always outwardly male to me. He had not changed so I did not feel like I had to make any decisions at that moment. Perhaps it was a coping mechanism to not address the big picture. The part of his story that impacted me most was his inability to have children. Being our third date, it was too early to even think about how his being transgender would affect the physical aspects of our relationship. I just knew he did not have the sperm to create a child if we wanted one. That night, I called my twin sister to begin to break the news to her but all I could get out was, "Todd told me that he can't have children." I did not tell her he was transgender.

During my business trip, I had time to reflect and evaluate what I wanted out of the relationship. My science background made me want to understand the facts first, then address my feelings later, so, I began to research about what it meant to be transgender. I think I compartmentalized the child-bearing part because I knew there were ways around it through adoption or having a donor.

I was away from Thursday to Tuesday for a conference, returned home for two nights and then was off again for four days to be a bridesmaid in my best friend's wedding. I saw Todd one night during my brief return home. While away, I found myself missing the person I had been dating. As we texted throughout my trip, I decided to take our relationship one day at a time. "Could I deal with it today?" I asked myself. Okay. The next day? Okay.

It was well into our relationship that we discussed his transition process, his past dating, his surgeries to that point, and what would be upcoming. That's probably when it really sunk in that Todd's transition would have a lifelong impact on our relationship. When the time came that we had to face the difficult stuff, I was in love with him and was committed to our relationship.

### Todd

Our relationship continued to grow and a year later, I realized that Katrina was "the one." I wanted to spend the rest of my life with her. I proposed, and we were married eighteen months later.

We arranged for the pastors from the church we attended to do our premarital. They were very affirming and agreed to perform the ceremony in Katrina's parents' hometown.

### *Katrina*

My family had really come to love Todd. They were thrilled he was going to be part of our family. However, I was so afraid that everything would change if they knew he was a trans man that I didn't tell them before we were married.

It was Thanksgiving, three years into our marriage, that we told my family that Todd was going to Serbia to have cosmetic surgery. The cost was prohibitive in the United States and our insurance would not cover it, so we had to go overseas. My mom heard "Serbia" and quickly did some research trying to find out more but she did not even consider that Todd was transgender. My family was still unaware.

Todd's parents came to Serbia with us to give support during surgery and after. His full reconstructive surgery required that we stay there for three weeks.

Shortly after our return to the United States, Todd had complications from the surgery and was admitted into the hospital. It was then that my family admitted that they knew about him. My twin sister said to me one day, "You know that we know." They had just put all the signs together.

Every year my family goes to the beach together. The first year, my mom asked what the scars were on Todd's chest. "Oh, he had to have some surgery." I explained. They asked no more questions. I just wanted them to figure it out on their own.

My family was hurt that I had not told them, not because Todd was trans but because they had known and loved him for eight years and we did not trust in that. "Why didn't you trust us to know?" They asked. They love Todd and have adjusted well to the news and have become intentional about learning about the LGBTQ community.

### *Todd's closing remarks*

I am thankful for my loving family and friends that have supported me through this journey. I spent a lot of energy trying to hide things in my life and it was a huge burden to carry.

This has been quite a learning experience for me. People have surprised me in their response to my story. For my grandfather, my change was a non-issue. Most of my dad's family were fine. There were a few, who continued to go to the nondenominational church that we left, that shunned us for a while. They were unkind and wouldn't show up for family gatherings. I remain very close to one of my cousins. Then, there is my mom's ninety-year-old cousin who lives in West Virginia on a farm. My mom didn't tell her for a while because she was afraid of her reaction. She responded with, "Okay," and has supported us with love. I have even taken my wife to meet her at my grandmother's request.

I have learned that we must be true to ourselves. So, if you are questioning your sexuality in any way, tell someone about it. There are medical services that can assist you as you work through your identity. There is hope and things will get better.

There will be people who will be unkind because of the position you have taken for your life, whether you are a member of the LGBTQ community or a supporter. I have never been physically attacked but I have been in fear of that happening because of comments that have been made to me. Be courageous and press on.

God has worked in many unusual ways in my life that have reminded me of just how much I am loved by Him. When I was struggling with the hatred from the church, God showed up to remind me once again. The interesting thing about scripture is that Jesus never said anything about this issue, but He did speak about love and strongly chastised those who lived outside of it. God loves each of us. Don't let anyone tell you otherwise.

*Todd works in information technology and lives in the northeast with his wife Katrina, who is a pharmacist. They have been happily married for four years.*

# Andrew

## Chapter 18

*Andrew recently graduated from an open and affirming Lutheran seminary in the mid-west that warmly welcomes people from the LGBTQ community. Each person from that seminary community goes there because of a desire for all people to come to know the deep love of God.*

*What Andrew has learned over the years is that God really is love and uses the circumstances of our lives to form us and build into us a capacity to communicate God's love to others. Every moment is truly eternal. Sometimes this eternity surrounds us with joy, and sometimes it sucks every ounce of hope out of us. Andrew finds beauty, serenity, and purpose in the triune God, who binds all of eternity together.*

### Andrew's Story

When I was six years old, my dad was incarcerated for robbing several banks. He was a witty, intelligent, sarcastic, introspective, self-loathing, alcoholic, manic depressive, who happened to be sober until I was six years old. He had serious addiction problems and became delusional. My dad would collect-call me periodically from prison, and I would visit him on a regular basis. My paternal aunt faithfully took me to visit him. She loved her brother, and what could have been a traumatic experience for me helped to form love and compassion instead. I really value that time with my dad.

My mom is an incredible person—loving, aloof, over-protective, hard-working, kind, genuine, and compassionate. She worked very hard to raise my sister, who was two years younger, and me, working 40 to 50-hour weeks as a respiratory therapist. Mom and dad divorced shortly before the armed robberies.

My childhood was marked by prison visits, with a struggling, overworked mother sustaining a middle-class lifestyle, a co-dependent, loving paternal aunt, and faith in an ever- forgiving, loving, gracious God.

There is much I can say about how being the child of a prisoner influenced me as a person. Reflecting on how it influenced my call to ordained ministry, I can say that I was forced to face the complexities of "right and wrong" from a young age. The questions, "Why must I suffer for my father's crimes? Why must children and loved ones of those incarcerated suffer?" is something with which I continue to wrestle when reflecting on my childhood and relationship with my father. I also had to face the privilege my skin color and ancestry given me; most of my ancestors had a college education and land. My family received better treatment from the prison guards than most visitors did, and we were almost always the only white, middle class folks there. In the words of one of my mentors, "your life has been marked with extreme privilege and extreme oppression." Simply put, this experience has given me a passion for justice that is restorative rather than oppressive. The justice Jesus

Christ preached about, lived for, died for, and most of all rose for.

I remember growing up feeling ashamed. My dad was in prison and my mom was a single parent but we received much support and encouragement from our extended family and that really helped. My sister and I would spend summers with our mom's sister at her home on the Jersey shore, and with my father's sister while we took swimming lessons. From time to time, my grandparents helped us to go on family vacations. I remember when we went to Disney World, my mom's cousin used his employee pass to take us into all the parks at no cost to us.

My sister and I were very close but fought a lot growing up. I was more aware of our financial situation of living paycheck to paycheck and she was not. When we were little we used to play together in the neighborhood. As we got older, we grew apart. Tension arose around how we chose to deal with our father's incarceration and addiction. I took out a lot of my anger on my sister. That still haunts me today to be honest; I think it still affects her.

My mom was raised Presbyterian and my dad Roman Catholic, so when they married they attended an Episcopal church. After the divorce, my mom started attending a Lutheran church closer to our home. The church had several rifts while we were there, conservatives versus the progressives. When I wrote a story about the birth of Jesus that was inaccurate, it didn't go well there so we moved on to the Episcopal church. We attended church once a month until I was confirmed.

I stopped Sunday school altogether when I did not get a particularly great response to my question on creationism. Our Sunday school teacher asked us how the big bang could be true because, "one cannot blow up a junkyard and create a Corvette." Me being raised a free thinker by my mom, pushed back. I asked, "But couldn't God? Why can't both be true?" After that, the teacher argued with me. When I told my mom about our exchange, she told me I didn't have to go to Sunday school anymore.

My faith formation really happened when I started going to a Lutheran summer camp at age ten. Everything changed after several summers spent at Mar-Lu-Ridge (MLR). There, I learned about and experienced a God that loved and accepted me for who I was. It was there I made my first life-long friends. At first, games, songs, Bible study, and team-building helped solidify these friendships. We expressed ourselves fully with each other there, sometimes this was euphoric and at other times it required patience and forgiveness. The natural beauty and the culture of shalom at Mar-Lu-Ridge opened our eyes to the divine presence that promises to be with us, especially when most vulnerable.

The love, faith, and individuality of my counselors inspired me to spend four summers as a counselor at MLR. I could make the holy almost tangible for my campers, like my counselors had for me. My eyes would always water during the closing worship because the new spark of faith and shalom in each of them was so moving. Mar-Lu-Ridge demonstrated the transformative power of Gospel-inspired shalom.

## Andrew

Growing up, my mom was overprotective of my sister and me. She always made sure to know where we were, and where we were going, and who we were with. If we ever violated her boundaries, there was always hell to pay.

Some of my happiest memories were with my extended family. We went to the beach every year with my mom's family. Our time together was filled with playing games, swimming, and gossip. I was very close to some of my cousins despite their being much older. Holiday meals were always very special at my mom's house. My cousins, uncle, and family friends come to join the celebration. We would drink, talk about politics, and catch up. Once I argued that I didn't want to teach children about Santa because he was fake, and my uncle, an agnostic, responded with, "I hate imagination". It's a running joke in our family now.

When I was eleven, my dad was released from prison and my sister and I had the opportunity to see him once a week. Visits were supervised by my aunt. I have fond memories of meals with my dad when he was home. He was an amazing cook and made incredible crab cakes.

Despite my unusual circumstances, I was just a regular kid. I loved to play outside in the woods and I also loved strategy games. Swimming was also fun. I was an athlete and played recreational soccer until in high school, then ran hurdles for the track team.

When I was twelve years old, I started to experience same-sex attraction. It was easy for me to ignore for a while because I was also attracted to girls. I consider myself bisexual. The homophobia in society prevented me from admitting what I was experiencing. I was raised by women that I highly respected. So, locker room talk was very offensive to me. It was difficult to know where I fit. So, I just stayed quiet about it.

High school was an interesting challenge. I did not date in high school because I did not know how. I remember hearing derogatory remarks about the gay community. "Faggot" or "gay" was yelled out but not toward me. These hurtful words were made in passing. I would hide to escape from hearing them.

My dad relapsed, while I was in high school, and he found himself back in prison. I was fifteen. He had a girlfriend that was just not good for him. This made it more challenging to have him directly involved in my life. He remained in prison until I was twenty-one.

I attended college with the goal of majoring in international affairs with development studies. I wanted to study to be a diplomat because I saw it as a career where my gifts for working with people and history, and my desire to help people, intersected. After six months, I became disillusioned with American foreign policy, and the dream of becoming a diplomat quickly floated from my brain. This led to a brief crisis, especially when the idea of ordained ministry floated into my head—a career path some of the church ladies tried to encourage.

Once I had reconciled the fact that this idea, which would set me apart from my friends and many in my generation, had taken root, I felt more and more called to nurture peoples' spirituality and create a culture of shalom. In those moments, the dreams of presiding over God's table and feeding God's people would take hold.

The thought of being a part of grassroots social justice movements, sustaining and renewing the spiritual life of a community, and standing in firm and vocal opposition to forces within the church that ignore the Gospel proclamation of shalom, was a signal that I had to seriously discern my vocation. With those thoughts racing through my head, I decided to send an innocent email inquiring about any internships relating to advocacy. I casually mentioned considering seminary. Next thing I knew, I had an email cc'd with about ten church leaders offering me all kinds of opportunities, except for an internship dealing with advocacy. It was through that interaction I was connected to Project Connect[1].

Project Connect provided with me a grant to work at Luther Place for one academic year to discern whether I felt called to parish ministry. I facilitated Bible studies on Ruth and Esther at N Street Village, was one of four adult leaders for a new youth group, taught senior high Sunday school, preached, organized a young-adult-led Good Friday service, served on the young adult leadership team and the Steinbruck Center steering committee, and got hands-on experience with church administration. I also had weekly spiritual direction from a mentor. The entire experience was valuable, but the most transformative experiences in terms of the call to ordained ministry were my spiritual direction and being a part of the women of N Street's Bible study.

---

[1] Project Connect is a ministry of the eastern cluster of Lutheran seminaries with the mission of assisting young adults with vocational discernment,

After the first few spiritual direction sessions, my mentor looked at me and said, "Andrew, you are a mystic." In subsequent sessions, we discussed articles and meditations by and for mystics. When I expressed the fact that I felt called to parish ministry she simply said, "The church needs good young leaders and mystics." That was the highest affirmation I received from my dear mentor. Facilitating Bible study at N Street transformed me because, with the help of my mentor, a space of mutuality was created where we learned from each other. It was in that room I learned how intimately connected empathy and perspective are, and how essential those are to understanding the Word and to our experience with God.

It was also in college that I felt the freedom to come out as bisexual. I dated two women before coming out but it did not amount to anything serious. I remember being attracted to guys, but I did not want to become a "college gay" (someone who comes out because of the freedom college allows), because I am bisexual. I did not want to publicly close myself off to being with women. I do remember going to a party where I got drunk and pinched a man's behind. My friend jokingly said that I was "bisexual." I called her later to tell her she was right. She also admitted to being bisexual.

I think it's important to note that same-sex relationships develop differently and have different dynamics than heterosexual relationships. I believe that this is because of the culture of homophobia. So, for a long time, I explored my sexuality in private because I feared being exposed. I found myself attracted to people, but I never voiced my feelings for someone unless I was sure they had feelings for me. I fear rejection, but I think that has more to do with my family dynamics than my sexuality.

I did try different ways to meet people, however. I enjoyed being a lifeguard at the gym, but nothing ever came out of my scanning the pool for "safety reasons." Eventually, I worked up the courage to meet someone online. We hung out, but we were not in a relationship. I wanted to explore the physical aspect more than the emotional. After we graduated, we just stopped talking, and I think we were both okay with that. I did fall in love with someone over the course of two months, but it ended abruptly when the guy "ghosted" me. We had a misunderstanding and he just stopped all communication. Eventually, he responded and told me to stop trying to contact him through text messages. It was a very painful experience. About two years later, he apologized but I have no plans to have any contact with him in the foreseeable future. Why invest my energy in someone who flippantly abandoned me?

After I graduated from college, I went to Hungary as part of Young Adults in Global Mission and lived alone there for a year. I decided to participate in this program because I wanted to discern how I was called to ministry in the world, to see if I could apply my academic knowledge about institutionalized racism in post-communist Europe, and to live out the accompaniment[2] model. Here, I taught English (language and Lutheran

---

[2] Accompaniment in the context of the ELCA Global Mission's way of doing "missionary" work.

religion in English) at a Lutheran school and was tasked with figuring out ways the Hungarian Lutheran church could facilitate a dialogue between non-Roma (the majority) and Roma in Hungary, in the context of my town, in partnership with organizations led by Roma for Roma. There, I learned that our world is complex, our problems are complex, and that God dwells in that complexity, promising that love and life win.

When I returned to the United States a year later, I started seminary. It was an open and affirming seminary that helped me to develop language around my sexuality. It was there that I had my broadest exposure to the LGBTQ community and developed some very close friends. Hatred was not welcome in that place. My experiences with God reminded me that God is love. We are all reflections of His image.

Coming out was more of a progression for me. First, I told my good friend Samantha that I was dating men, when the conversation arose. She was so affirming. Then, I started telling people in my seminary. It was a little more complicated to explain what bisexual meant. That changed as I got more experience telling my story. Bisexuals can often be discriminated against because it has been thought to be a stepping stone to being gay or straight. Many people do not understand that one can be attracted to both sexes.

I was twenty-one when my dad was released from prison because of health reasons at age sixty. He had been hospitalized after a fall and had back problems. I saw him periodically but at age twenty-four, I became very frustrated with him and did not talk to him for a year.

After a year of no communication we reconciled, and I am so glad we did. My dad died six months ago from an aneurism. He just collapsed one day and he was gone.

I really did not come out to my family until I started dating my partner, Eric, three years ago. My mom responded that she "had a hunch." She wanted me to be protected. My dad was accepting but always referred to my partner as my "friend." My stepdad was uncomfortable at first but came around later. My sister was my greatest ally. She had done gender studies in college in her study of statistics and psychology, so she was very supportive.

There have been a few people in my life that have had a profound impact on the person I have become. I am grateful for the influence my mom, dad, and aunt have had in my life. We have walked life's journey through the joy and the pain. I have learned much about love from my experience with visiting my dad in prison. I do know that despite his choices, he never stopped loving me. My aunt faithfully strived to make that relationship continue. What a gift. My mom was always devoted to giving me the best life that she could. I am amazed at her strength and courage. She has loved me consistently well. The faithfulness of my family and friends has made me realize that I could have come out sooner. Through them, I have experienced God's love in a new way.

My call to ministry has developed over time. Before realizing that I felt called to ministry, I would have written off my time spent at my home church and the congregation there as insignificant. Now, I see it as the place that has been a steadfast support for me, a constant presence on my spiritual journey. It was the place where my Christian journey began in the waters of my baptism and is a place of constant affirmation of my call to ministry. My call is to proclaim the manifold and mysterious ways God is alive in this world through my words, and my sharing of the ancient sacraments of church and tangible grace with all who desire them.

As far as sexuality is concerned, we must remember that we are made in God's image and should never be ashamed of who we are. He loves us no matter what. Feel the freedom to question and explore, always remembering that we are loved.

*Andrew graduated from seminary in spring 2017 and has been called to pastor a congregation in the Lutheran church. He lives in the mid-west near his partner of three years, Eric.*

# *Now,*
# *who do you say they are?*

## Chapter 19

I am profoundly thankful to each person who humbly shared the intimate details of their lives for this book. I hope that my written words have reflected the beauty of each incredible account. It was heartwarming to sit face to face with each person—to see them laugh, to hear of their heartbreak, to share their tears, and to hear how love has been an ointment to their soul. Ultimately, their hopes and dreams are for something as basic as you and I hope for and dream about...love.

God was powerfully present as I listened to each person share their unique, personal life stories. I have been changed through this experience. There were many moments that I was completely undone by the strength and courage that they demonstrated through the pain and suffering they endured. I found myself weeping and praying for God to reveal Himself, to bring healing and hope, to bless their lives with love. They are beautiful! Every one of them has captured my heart, and I truly love them.

Each of these stories expresses a deep desire to be known and loved. The "secret" that they carried was a tremendous weight of denial of self, and most of them carried it alone. Not one person awoke one morning and said, "I would like to be gay today." None of them wanted to bring hardship upon their families or themselves. None of them wanted to flee from the churches they loved and served because they were not accepted there. Each wanted to live as himself...herself...authentically. Members of the LGBTQ community are no different than anyone else.

You may have found some of these stories difficult to read. Not too long ago, it was unheard of to come out as LGBTQ. The pressure of keeping such a secret prevented a person from having true community. Their lives were often lived in the shadows or the alternative was...fully living a lie. Each person was seeking to be loved.

Today, many churches present a message that says that if you are from the LGBTQ community, you are mistaken about your identity. You should try to change who you believe you are and live a celibate life. They offer suggestions for types of therapy, many of which have been outlawed because of the serious adverse effects. Many individuals have succumbed to depression or suicide because of such so-called therapy. Isn't this asking a person to become someone they're not? To lie? Isn't this implying that if you do not change, you are not loved by God? What about God's unconditional love? For many years, people in the LGBTQ community have judged themselves and have tried to change without success. When they finally embrace their identity, they continue to hear the hurtful messages from the church. Rather than risk the continued hurt and judgment, they turn away from this conditionally loving "God" the church presents. It breaks my heart to think that the church itself is turning people from God. Even straight millennials are leaving the church in droves because of its intolerance and lack of love toward others. The "God" represented by the church is one that is unrecognizable to them. Rather, they seek the One True God...a loving God. This has huge ramifications for the future of the church. It will not take very long for the church to cease to exist without the young people to carry it forward.

When you are an LGBTQ person of faith and choose to embrace your sexuality and become an open member of the LGBTQ community, there are three possible options. First, you can flee from the church and leave God behind. Second, you can flee the church and practice your faith in isolation. Or third, you can cling to God and courageously share your life with the church. The way a church treats members of this community will directly affect the option they choose. What do you believe is God's greatest desire?

You have heard over and over in these stories, "If I would have known how my family and friends would have accepted me, I would have come out sooner." My response to that is more of a question than a statement. How can we keep the lines of communication open with our loved ones so that they feel free to share anything with us?

If you are gay and living a secret life, be courageous. Please, tell someone. You know how weighty and isolating it is to carry this alone, but it does not need to be that way. Start with someone you know loves you, and whom you trust completely. You will find that the people who truly love you will continue to do so. Some adjustment time might be necessary, but love will be victorious. It always is. It has probably taken you years to adjust to your true self. Allow some time for others to process the news as well.

If you are a parent, keep the lines of communication open with your son or daughter. Remember the words of I Corinthians 13:4-6 and claim them for the sake of the relationship with your child:

> *Love is patient, love is kind. It does not envy, it does not boast, it is not proud. It does not dishonor others, it is not self-seeking, it is not easily angered, it keeps no record of wrongs. Love does not delight in evil but rejoices with the truth. It always protects, always trusts, always hopes, always perseveres. Love never fails.*

Love is the answer. When Jesus was asked what the greatest commandment was, He responded with:

> *'The most important one,' answered Jesus, 'is this: "Hear, O Israel: the Lord our God, the Lord is one. Love the Lord your God with all your heart and with all your soul and with all your mind and with all your strength." The second is this: "Love your neighbor as yourself." There is no commandment greater than these.'*—Mark 12:29-31

Parents, love your child by listening to their story. It has taken great courage for them to come out to you. They have a life you know nothing about and they want to share it with you. Ask them to tell you their story. You may find that it answers many of your questions. They have probably been wrestling for years with this identity; don't try to explain their experiences away or shame them. In other words, don't do what I did when my son first approached me.

I have replayed the tape in my head several times through the years. When my son shared with me what he was feeling, I tried to explain it away. My fears prevented me from truly engaging with him and his story. I could have prevented so much pain for him. It grieves my heart to think about that.

If your children were raised in the church, there is probably nothing you can say to them about their sexuality and their faith that they have not wrestled with already. Many have struggled with same-sex attraction for years before coming out. I encourage you to just love them and pray for God to reveal His best for them. Trust God. He loves your child even more than you do.

When my son came out after college, he had been living a passionate life of faith. As I expressed my greatest concerns for him, he said something profound to me: "You're going to have to trust in my relationship with God." He was right. So, I decided to do just that. Not only did I choose to trust in his relationship with God, but I intentionally entrusted God with the sweet grown child whom I loved. It was hard, but all along the way, God has reminded me of His love for our son and our family.

If you are a member of the church and are trying to understand the LGBTQ community, I ask you this: Is it possible for people to coexist in the church and have different beliefs? Can people disagree on issues and live in harmony? Jesus was very clear about how we are to live in relationship. Can we allow God to do the transformation? We are all in the process...all on the journey. Far too often I have seen churches divide over issues because people thought differently from one another. Does it have to be so? It is time for the church to teach congregations how to love and respect people who have different views.

You know the old saying, "Sticks and stones can hurt my bones, but names will never hurt me?" Well, it's not true. Words do hurt, and we need to learn to be sensitive to others with our words. Much of the time we are totally unaware of how what we say might wound another person. For instance, I remember when my husband and I were gathered with a group of people to inform them of why we were leaving the church. An older woman prayed such an offensive and judgmental prayer that after the gathering was over, one of the elders came up to apologize to us. Our words do matter. They can be used to encourage someone and build them up or to tear people apart and alienate them. Which do you think is God's desire?

Even the most innocent joking can inflict serious pain. When our son was in the process of discernment about his sexuality, after college, he started attending a Bible study at a church our former church had planted. He was enjoying the group until one night when a snide remark was made that involved someone "being gay." He never went back to that group again.

During that same time, we had offered to share our home with a family from our church who was living overseas and visiting the U.S. for a few months. A week into their visit, the teenage son made a comment about something being "gay" while our son was home for a visit. It was highly offensive and very hurtful, but the boy had no idea what he had done. Sadly, neither did his parents. They did not stay with us much longer after that incident.

You may be thinking, "It's one thing to accept people and use kind words, but how do we love people whom we don't understand?" There is only one way…by getting to know them on a personal level. The greatest change to my heart was when the LGBTQ community became personal for me through my son's story. For that I am truly grateful. As a result, I have been inspired to reach beyond myself and to be intentional about hearing people's stories, to know them on a deeper level. That is when you begin to love.

It may feel safer to be with people who have the same beliefs as you, but I don't believe that this is how God desires for us to live. It certainly is not how Jesus lived. Are you willing to step outside of your safe life to see Jesus working in the lives of people who are unlike yourself? I think that you will find that they are not as different as you expected.

Allow yourself to get to know God in a deeper way. He is working all around us through all the people of this world. God has much to reveal to us about Himself through those who are unlike us. He is speaking. Do you hear His desire for all people?

I pray that your heart has been opened through the stories of this book to view the LGBTQ community differently. Even if your position on this issue has not changed, I hope that a deeper understanding allows you to express a posture of love as you relate to this community of people going forward.

I hope that the stories shared here have shown you that sexuality is only a small part of who people from the LGBTQ community are. They are kind and compassionate men and women. They have gifts and talents that they share with the world. They are our social workers, doctors, nurses, therapists, emergency medical team, engineers, teachers, lawyers, business men and women, pastors, flight attendants, factory workers, service men and women, postal workers, artists...and on and on. They have families who love them. And more importantly, they are children of the living God, created by Him in His image and He loves them deeply.

Over the years, God has taught me that sometimes we will not have answers to our deepest questions...not on this earth anyway. And I have come to believe that the answers are not what we are to be seeking. What God desires most is for us to know, love, and trust Him with every part of our lives...the joys and the challenges...and to know and love others as He does...unconditionally.

*Our younger son, Jeremy, is currently completing a PhD in social work, specializing in LGBTQ research, and has shared his research all over the world. He is married to a wonderful man, Leandro, whom we adore and who is an amazingly talented writer and film director.*

*Now, who do you say they are?*

Our older son, Jamey, is a brilliant electrical engineer and lives nearby with his beautiful wife, Katie, and our four adorable grandchildren.

My wonderful husband, Jim, and I are exploring new ways in which we can be used for the greater good of the Kingdom of God. Justice issues are important to us. We will see where God takes us next.

# *Resources*

## Books:

Baldock, Kathy. Walking the Bridgeless Canyon: Repairing the Breach Between the Church and the LGBT Community, Canyonwalker Press, 2014.

Belge, K., Bieschke, M., Robinson, C., Queer: The Ultimate LGBTQ Guide for Teens, 2011.

Bigner, J., and Wetchler J., Handbook for LGBT-Affirmative Couple and Family Therapy, 2012.

Blumenfield, Warren J, editor, Homophobia: How We All Pay the Price, Boston: Beacon Press, 1992.

Brill, S. and Pepper, R, The Transgender Child ,2008.

Coles, Gregory. Single Gay Christian: A Personal Journey of Faith and Sexual Identity. IVP Books, 2017.

Ehrensaft, D., Gender Born, Gender Made: Raising Healthy Gender-Nonconforming Children. 2011.

Fakhrid-Deen, T, and COLAGE. Let's Get This Straight: The Ultimate Handbook for Youth with LGBTQ Parents, 2010.

Gray, M. L., Out in the Country: Youth, Media, and Queer Visibility in Rural America, Intersections: Trans disciplinary Perspectives on Genders and Sexualities, 2009.

Krieger, I., Helping Your Transgender Teen: A Guide for

Parents, 2011.

Lee, Justin. Torn: Rescuing the Gospel from the Gays-vs-Christians Debate. Jericho Books, 2013.

Levithan, D., and Merrell, B. The Full Spectrum, 2006

Mallon, G., LGBTQ Youth Issues: Practical Guide for Youth Workers Serving Lesbian, Gay, Bisexual, Transgender and Questioning Youth, 2010.

Miceli, Melinda, Standing Out, Standing Together: The Social and Political Impact of Gay-Straight Alliances, 2005.

Miner, Rev. Jeff and Connoley, Rev. John Tyler. The Children Are Free. Reexamining the Biblical Evidence on Same-Sex Relationships. LifeJourney Press, 2002.

Pompei, V., LGBTQ Youth: An Educator's Guide, 2012.

Riggle, E. D. B., and Rostosky, S., A Positive View for LGBTQ: Embracing Identity and Cultivating Well-Being, Rwoman Littlefield, 2011.

# Websites and Phone Numbers:

### GLBT National Resource Hotline

1-888-THE-GLNH (1-888-843-4564). Confidential peer counseling and information on local resources. Open Monday through Friday 4-12 PM EST; Saturday 12-5pm EST.

### Just the Facts: Primer Booklet on Sexual Orientation
https://www.apa.org/pi/lgbt/resources/just-the-facts.aspx

An information booklet designed for principals, educators, and school personnel on sexual orientation and youth. This booklet was created in response to the recent rise in sexual orientation conversion therapy and those beliefs being wanted to be shared in school settings.

**National AIDS Information Line**

1-800-CDC-INFO for HIV and AIDS information 24 Hours a Day, Seven days a week

**National Runaway Switchboard**

1-800-RUNAWAY (1-800-786-2929)

The National Runaway Switchboard is a toll-free crises line operated by Chicago's Metro-Help. It operates twenty-four hours a day, year-long, and is designed to serve the needs of youth and their families. The phone lines are staffed by trained volunteers who use crisis intervention and active listening techniques to help callers identify their problems, explore options, and develop a plan of action. Their services are secular (non-religious), nonjudgmental, and non-directive. Volunteers try to give callers factual information and confront irrational perceptions and solutions. They also offer message-relays (communication between runaways and parents without disclosing location of runaway) and referrals to over 8,000 social service agencies nationwide.

**National Suicide Prevention Lifeline**

1-800-273-TALK (8255) English

1-888-628-9454 Spanish

http://www.suicidepreventionlifeline.org/

Crisis hotline and online chat available

**Our Daughters & Sons/Nuestras Hijas y Nuestros Hijos**

**Questions & Answers for Parents of Gay, Lesbian & Bisexual People**

https://www.pflag.org/sites/default/files/Our%20Trans%20Loved%20Ones.pdf (English)

https://www.pflag.org/sites/default/files/Nuestras_hijas.pdf (Spanish)

**Resource Guide to Coming Out**

https://www.hrc.org/resources/resource-guide-to-coming-out

A PDF electronic guide to assist in the process in coming out as a LGBTQ individual. It offers advice and guidance while acknowledging the real emotions and difficulties one experiences while coming out.

**STD Info Line**

1-800-227-8922 For STI Information, Monday-Friday, 8:00am – 11:00pm Eastern Time

**Teenline**

www.teenlineonline.org

(310) 855-HOPE (4673) or (800) TLC-TEEN (852-8336) (toll-free in California only). Helpline that offers teen to teen support and guidance. Open 6pm to 10pm Pacific Time, every night. Texting also offered.

**The Trevor Project, Inc.** thetrevorproject.org. 2017

1-866-4-U-TREVOR (1-866-488-7386) The Trevor Project is focused on crisis intervention and suicide prevention to LGBTQ youth. Provides several services including a helpline: The Trevor Lifeline, chat/communication services—Ask Trevor and Trevor Chat— supports a social networking site for LGBTQ youth and supporters. Also, is involved in public policy advocacy and research. The Trevor Project is not just a suicide hotline; they can help with all kinds of issues.

**The Gay Christian Network,** gaychristian.net. 2017

**Youth-Focused Hotline**

1-800-246-PRIDE or (1-800-246-7743) www.glnh.org/talkline